A Place
Prepared

Stories from the lives of men and women who heard
God's voice, stepped into His plan and found His place.

GLORIA KEARNEY

AMBASSADOR

BELFAST, NORTHERN IRELAND
GREENVILLE, USA

By the same author:
Sing in the Shadow published 1999
Special Moments published 2000

ISBN 1 84030 134 1

Ambassador Publications
a division of
Ambassador Productions Ltd.
Providence House
Ardenlee Street,
Belfast,
BT6 8QJ
Northern Ireland
www.ambassador-productions.com

Emerald House
427 Wade Hampton Blvd.
Greenville
SC 29609, USA
www.emeraldhouse.com

Mission Africa
14 Glencregagh Court,
Belfast,
BT6 0PA
Northern Ireland
www.missionafrica.org.uk

Foreword

This little book is a treasure and a pleasure to read. It traces a period of 70 years in which the Church was planted among the Lobi, Birifor and Dagaari peoples of south western Burkina Faso in West Africa by recounting the stories of two couples involved in this work of God.

What a moving story it is to read of God's dealings with Stanley and Alice Benington, pioneer missionaries of the Qua Iboe Fellowship, and how he formed them into instruments for the ultimate breakthrough of the Gospel in a people steeped in idolatry and witchcraft. The cost of obedience and for fruitfulness was high. Yet there is the joy of reading how God brought Lobi, Birifor and even Muslims to faith in Christ through this obedience and in answer to much prayer. Then the book moves on to pick up the story of Jeremy and Rachel Nash as they embarked on the same costly process in a neighbouring people, the Dagaari and, in this, there is the challenge that a new generation of prayer supporters take up the challenge of seeing further advances for the Kingdom among the less-reached peoples of Burkina Faso and beyond.

This book is also a testimony of sweet and fruitful cooperation between different mission agencies that was an essential for the birthing of this West African Church. I was encouraged by reading how even I personally have played a small part in the process!

Buy it and be blessed and encouraged, give it to others, that they too might be blessed and encouraged! May there be others who also find a place prepared by God in some challenging part of the world where the Gospel light must yet shine.

Patrick Johnstone
WEC International
Author, *Operation World*

This book is dedicated to my
new granddaughter, Freya Catherine.
May she too hear God's voice and step into His plan.

It was never intended that this book should be either a history or a biography. It is, quite simply, what it claims to be on the front cover - stories from the lives of Stanley and Alice Benington and Jeremy and Rachel Nash. Through these stories it attempts to trace the beginnings of the work of the Qua Iboe Fellowship (now Mission Africa) in Burkina Faso and to show how God prepared a place and a people and the servants who, in obedience to His call, brought His Gospel to that part of West Africa.

My thanks are due to the following:

My longsuffering family, who encouraged me, once again, to keep on writing;

The other three members of my prayer quartet, who often had to pray for motivation and inspiration;

John Cardoo, Jean Corbett and other members of the Qua Iboe family, who supported me in this rather daunting task;

The Nash family and the WEC team in Burkina Faso, who looked after me so well during my fact-finding trip and who so patiently answered my questions;

Rachel Nash, her mother Pauline and her brother, Paul, who provided all the lovely illustrations;

Jack Robertson, Mady Vaillant, Brian Woodford, and Andre and Yvonne Wilson, who helped to supply some of the details that were needed;

Stanley and Alice's children, Russell, Maurice and June, who kindly agreed to read the manuscript and comment on it;

Paul Fleming, who so willingly proofread the first draft;

I also wish to acknowledge the Deputy Keeper of the Records, the Public Records Office of Northern Ireland and the Qua Iboe Fellowship who granted me access to Mission archives.

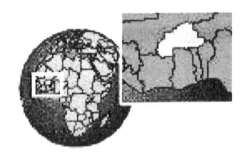

List of Contents

PROLOGUE
A White Man and His Wife

The blackness of an African night had long since descended on the little village of Bouroum-Bouroum. Here and there the village fires were still smoking and the spicy smells of the evening meal still hung in the air. Tigite climbed onto the low roof of his house. It was too hot to sleep inside. He lay down and settled himself on his cloth, sighing contentedly.

Everything was ready. His wives had been working hard all day, making beer and preparing food. He had spent many hours collecting all the sacrifices that would be necessary for the ceremonies. He felt the excitement rise up inside him again – tomorrow would be the best day of his life!

The chiefs of the nearby villages were coming. The witch doctors would all be there too. By the end of the celebrations and ceremonies tomorrow, Tigite would be a fully-fledged witch doctor. For Tigite, this was a dream come true – the pinnacle of success. Everyone would look up to him now – treat him with respect, maybe even fear. What power he would have! How proud his family would be. He fell asleep with a smile on his face.

Some time later he woke with a start and looked around in confusion.

"What am I doing on the ground?" he wondered. "How did that happen?"

Coming to the conclusion that he must have rolled off the roof in his sleep, he quickly climbed back up and was soon asleep again. The second time it happened, he muttered angrily,

"I'll never get to sleep if this keeps happening. Why tonight of all nights?"

The third time that he fell to the ground below, he was left in no doubt about what was happening. A voice spoke to him, calling him by name,

"Tigite, destroy your idols. The day for sacrifices has passed. I am going to send a white man and his wife into your village to tell you My way."

Tigite shook with fear as he looked around in the darkness to try to see who was speaking to him. What power could this be? He knew what the power of a spirit was like but he had never encountered power like this before. What power could throw a man off his roof, not once, but three times? What power could speak so clearly? What mighty being knew him by name?

He lay, waiting for the voice to speak again, but he heard no more. Sleep fled from him that night as he contemplated the immensity of what he had been asked to do. Could he really burn his idols? He and his family depended on them for their health, for good crops, for the rains, for protection. What if the voice was wrong? Could he give up the prestige that being a witch doctor would bring? He knew of no one who had refused this high honour. How would the witch doctors react? They might well decide that he deserved to die. Burning his idols was such a drastic step. Maybe he should wait until the promised white man actually came?

When dawn finally came, however, he knew that he had really no choice. The visitation from the One whom he now considered to be God, the Supreme Being, had made such an impression on him, he could not disobey His voice.

Tigite rose early and by the time the rest of the villagers were stirring, the smoke was already beginning to rise from the pile of idols outside his house. Now all he had to do was wait for the white man and his wife..........

Not many men in their lifetime have the privilege of walking in the prophecy given to another, especially when they live thousands of miles apart and have never met.

Stanley Benington was such a man.........

.... together with Alice, his wife,

he fulfilled the double promise of Tigite's visitation.

1

BOATS, BITES and BABIES

The great steamer slowly forged its relentless path through the waves as it made its way north along the west coast of Africa. The tall, slim missionary and his wife stood at the rail, enjoying the sunshine and the cool breezes. They were returning to Northern Ireland from Nigeria and were looking forward to a time of rest and refreshment after a busy tour serving the Lord with the Qua Iboe Mission. As was customary, Stanley and Alice had been booked on a cargo boat for their journey home and they spent many happy hours, sitting on the deck, watching the distant shore glide by.

"It all looks so beautiful," said Alice, as she gazed at the low-lying coastline. "The palm trees along the shore….. the white breakers on the sandy beach……… the blue, misty hills beyond….. it all looks idyllic."

"I wonder who lives there," pondered Stanley, "I wonder if they have ever heard the Gospel? It's strange to think that we have sailed up and down along this coastline many times and yet we know nothing about the people groups who live there."

"Except what the sailors tell us," laughed Alice, "and maybe we shouldn't believe everything we hear from them!"

"Yes," agreed Stanley, "they do tell the most marvellous stories. They only know about the ports and the dockside streets, of course. I would love to know about the people who live in the little villages of the interior. I wonder if they are living in darkness and cannibalism as the people of Qua Iboe were when our missionaries first went there?"

"They probably are," Alice said sadly. "I haven't heard of anyone working among them. I wonder how long it will be before someone goes to them with the message of Jesus?"

"It has been amazing to see the difference the Gospel can make in a few years." Stanley's face lit up as he spoke. "I first went to Nigeria in 1917, when I was 24 years old, so I've been there now for 13 years and it has just been wonderful to see what God has done in that time. There's a native church in almost every village of the people group, the Church has been properly constituted and it has its own native ministry."

"Yes indeed," said Alice, "there are some very fine men serving the Church."

Stanley looked out across the sea once more.

"Maybe sometime we'll have the opportunity to find out more about the people groups over there. It could be that someone at home knows about the situation in those countries. I must try to get some information."

Stanley and Alice Benington came from Northern Ireland. Stanley had been brought up first of all in Lisburn, where his father was a teacher in Friends' School. They then moved to Moira, to Brookfield School, a school that provided training for farm labourers and servants. His father was appointed the head teacher in the school.

Even before he was born, his parents had prayed that he would become a missionary in Africa and their prayers were answered despite the fact that Stanley himself was more interested in South America. He used to argue with his mother, in a good-natured way, about the respective needs of the two continents.

Then his mother invited him to go with her to the Qua Iboe annual meeting in 1914.

"Are you going alone?" he asked.

"Yes, I'm going alone," was the reply.

"Alright, I'll come," said Stanley.

The Lord spoke very clearly to him at that meeting -

"Qua Iboe is your place, the place that I have called you to."

He had argued with his mother but there was to be no arguing with God. He wrote to the mission soon afterwards and, three years later, having made a determined struggle to pass the matriculation examination and to learn French, he arrived in Qua Iboe on 11th November 1917.

Despite being only twenty-four years of age, he was put in charge of a Centre with eighty-two churches and a large unevangelised area. Looking back on those early years, he would later remark –

"I wasn't fit for it but the Lord wanted me there, not so much that I might work for Him as that he might work in me and do things in me that He couldn't do at home. That is always the aim of the Lord in putting us in different places – He wants to develop our characters."

Many of his early experiences were certainly character building – others were just painful! One of the latter was his first encounter with driver ants. He liked to join the local Christians each Friday at his first station, Mbiuto, for their prayer meeting, which was held an hour after sunset. Night fell swiftly in Nigeria and a short time after sunset, it was totally dark. Stanley enjoyed the half-mile walk with the houseboys from his house to the little church, guided along the path by the light of the lantern carried by the boys. The evenings were warm, the crickets sang loudly in the bush and the night sky sparkled with the light of thousands of stars.

One Friday, as usual, he sat up at the front beside the missionary who had been staying with him to help him settle in. Stanley listened to the men as they prayed, recognising their passion for God even though he couldn't understand the words they were saying. Suddenly, during one of the prayers, he felt a little bite. He slapped his hand down to kill whatever had bitten him and felt another bite, then another. Within a moment he felt as though he was being bitten all over and had to get up quickly and run outside so that he could remove his trousers and get rid of the ants that were crawling all over him. He couldn't understand why the bites were so painful or why they didn't fall off when he flicked his hand at them but his missionary friend explained later that the ants he had encountered were driver ants.

"They have a fierce bite," he said, "and you have to actually pull them off because they sink their mandibles into your skin."

When he next met them, he knew enough to give them a wide berth. It was very early in the morning and the boys came running in, in a great state of excitement.

"Etubom, come quickly, there are ants in the kitchen!"

"Well," said Stanley, wondering what all the fuss was about, "get a straw brush and brush them out."

"Oh we can't do that – they're driver ants."

What a sight met his eyes when he went to investigate. There were great seething masses of ants hanging everywhere like swarms of bees. They were hanging from different parts of the ceiling. They covered one wall entirely. The boys had left something in an open tin, the ants had smelt it and had come for it. The entire colony of ants filled the kitchen. Stanley knew what would happen if he tried to touch them. There was nothing they could do except wait until they had all passed through. It took the whole day and Stanley watched from a safe distance, marvelling at these amazing creatures. After they had investigated the food, they arranged themselves into rows of four or five ants and marched out of the kitchen in a long ribbon. On the outside of this long column, the soldier ants kept running back and forth, guarding the column from trouble. He had always been interested in nature but these tiny creatures were among the most fascinating he had ever seen.

His belief in the power of prayer was tested at an early stage. Although he had no medical training, the people often looked to him for help when they were sick. There was a dispensary near his house and he used to go down there in the morning if he was not travelling anywhere. He saw some very distressing cases and did what he could to help. The previous missionary had left some medical books and Stanley studied these to help him decide on which treatment to use. When Asian 'flu' struck the area, many people died and Stanley had to resort to making up all sorts of medicine when the supplies in the dispensary ran out. He could refuse no one in case people thought he had favourites.

Around this time there was a knock at the door one night.

"Yes, who is there?" he shouted.

The callers gave their names and Stanley went to the door to enquire why they had come so late at night.

"Please, Sir," came the despairing cry, "my wife she no fit born baby!"

"Well," said Stanley, "I don't know anything about babies."

"Will you just give her some medicine?" the man pleaded.

"Take her down to the empty house and I'll bring her something," Stanley promised.

He got dressed and frantically searched his medical books.

"Babies................. how to 'born' babies."

He could find nothing at all on the subject but came across a drug called 'ergot' which promised to do all sorts of good things so he got a dose of ergot and brought it down to the woman. He gave it to her and then returned to his own house.

He began walking round and round the table in the hall, the central part of the house, praying that God would intervene in the situation. He went back again to consult the books, which he had left lying open on the table. His eye was drawn to the following instruction:

"On no account should ergot be given until the baby has been delivered."

"Oh my," he groaned, "there, I've done it. Well, Lord, I did my best and I pray that thou wilt overrule and undertake and deliver this good woman."

He knew that he could do nothing more at this stage so he went to bed, content just to leave the situation with the Lord.

At about three or four o'clock in the morning, he was wakened by another thump at the door.

"Oh dear," he thought, "here it is now."

He went to the door, prepared to hear the worst and to sympathise with the man on the loss of his wife, but he was amazed to hear the man yelling,

"Thank you, thank you Massa, my wife she go born child!"

He went down to the room and there was a beautiful little baby lying on the mud floor. A midwife was throwing cold water over it and Stanley thought that if it survived the shock of that, it would be a strong, healthy baby. That was the first of many medical emergencies where the successful outcome owed more to the power of prayer and Stanley's faith in God than to any medical skill on his part.

2

CONFRONTING EGBO

Other character building experiences took an entirely different form. Soon after he arrived at his first station, Mbiuto, some young men from a town about fifty or sixty miles away, came to visit him. They had waited in the early morning with the rest of the crowd outside Stanley's house. Men from many different villages had come with the same purpose – to plead with the white man for a "teacha". News of the Gospel was spreading rapidly and many were hungry to have someone come to their village to tell them about Jesus.

Their own purpose was slightly different. They wanted Stanley's help.

"We have asked the chiefs of our village to give us a piece of land on which to build a church but they have refused," they said. "Would you come and try to persuade the chiefs?"

It was, in Stanley's opinion, too good an opportunity to miss so he agreed to make the journey. He had an old motorbike at that time and he packed as much as he could into the carrier, then set off with one of his helpers riding pillion. Stanley wasn't used to riding through deep sand and the motorbike began to swerve wildly as they travelled through a clearing where the sand had been washed into the path by the heavy rains. As soon as he reached the edge of the clearing, he shouted over his shoulder, "Are you alright?"

There was no reply, so he stopped the motorbike and looked back. All he could see of the boy were his heels sticking up in the bush!

They did make it safely to the town and the young men who had invited them were very excited to see them, running around in circles in their determination to make them welcome. One of them brought out an old camp chair and put it on the veranda of his house. He had obviously had dealings with white men before and knew what they would like. Next to appear was a little table, covered by a cloth, on which he carefully placed a glass and a bottle of Scotch!

"Would you like to drink after your hot journey?" he enquired politely.

"Well," Stanley replied, "I would like a drink very much but I don't drink this kind of drink."

The young men looked disappointed, then moved away to discuss the situation. After a few moments a boy from the town went tearing off on his bicycle, only to return with another bottle of whiskey – a different brand. Their disappointment knew no bounds when Stanley refused to drink it too.

They tried again, this time sending another boy clambering up the smooth trunk of a nearby palm tree. There was a dull thud as a coconut landed in the sand. It was quickly opened and Stanley was relieved to be able to accept the traditional drink of coconut milk. The young men were pleased that their hospitality had been accepted and Stanley was happy to have his thirst quenched.

"The chiefs are ready," someone called and they all set out for the agreed meeting place, the Egbo playground. The scene was set for the palaver.

The Egbo was the most powerful and the most popular secret society in the area where Qua Iboe worked at that time. They ruled by fear and secrecy and their decisions were rarely questioned. At the "time of Egbo" every year, they would meet for celebrations, during which the men would wear fantastic masks, some shaped like the heads of birds, others with mechanical mouths which could open and shut. Their bodies were greased and blackened and they wore grass skirts. No one could tell who they were for they spoke in squeaky voices in an attempt to sound like spirits.

Very often, as the festivities progressed, the evil spirits they worshipped would take possession of them and frail old men who could barely walk in normal circumstances would spend hours in the circle dancing in honour of the Egbo drums. Stanley knew a little of the satanic power of these men and as he walked into the circle that was known as the Egbo playground, he wondered what the rest of the day would bring.

He sat with the other men on the trunk of a tree and gazed around. In the centre of the circle sat an enormous idol, the "god of heaven" and the "god of earth". It was bigger than any he had ever seen before and in his heart he breathed a prayer of thanksgiving that the God he served, the True God was greater than any idol man could make.

He and the young men who had invited him waited and waited and for a long time nothing happened. He knew, of course, that he was being made to wait so that he would understand the importance of those who were keeping him waiting! The chiefs were making the most of this opportunity to show their disdain for the white man.

When the men of the town did begin to gather, Stanley was rather concerned to see that they were surreptitiously trying to hide their long knives in the bush that was just beyond the circle. They sat down on the raised edge of the circle and they too waited for a long time. After about an hour, the chiefs finally arrived. Stanley watched them with interest. Some of them were old, wizened-up men, others were tall, proud men and all of them were dressed in an amazing array of second hand clothes that had been sent out from England – soldiers' clothes, all kinds of garments and the most wonderful hats.

They ignored Stanley, going straight to the idol to make an offering. They poured out some palm wine into a calabash, then spilled it along the ground at the foot of the idol. As they did so, they called out,

"God of heaven, god of earth, deliver us from this man who has come among us."

It could hardly have been called a warm welcome! After a while they sat down.

"We are ready. Have you anything to say?"

After the customary greetings, Stanley told them about the young men who had asked for his help.

"They would like you to give them a place where they can build a school. They want to learn to read and write. They do not wish to live any longer like goats, without developing their powers in any way. They also want to know about God and about Jesus Christ."

His words were greeted by silence. Then, very slowly, the oldest chief pulled himself to his feet and began speaking, punctuating his words with occasional thumps on the ground from the long staff in his hand. He too began with the usual polite greetings and discussed the matter quite calmly. He spoke for a long time, then suddenly started shouting in a loud voice.

"As long as I live," he thundered, thumping the ground with his staff, "as long as the chiefs of this town live, we will never have a school in this town!"

At these words, the men of the town, who had been sitting all around the circle, jumped up, ran to the bush, seized their knives and surrounded Stanley and his friends.

"Is this how it is going to end?" thought Stanley, as he looked into their angry faces.

"Now get out of our town," yelled the chief. "If you don't get out and get out quickly, we'll kill you! And don't ever come back!"

Deciding that this was not a good time to argue, Stanley and his boy got up, bowed politely to the chiefs and greeted both the chiefs and the people. Then very gingerly, Stanley pushed the boy in front of him and began to walk out of the circle. The angry crowd followed them, shouting and gesticulating. Although he didn't actually feel afraid, he would never forget the strange, creepy sensation in his back as he walked on out of the town.

The triumph of the chiefs was short-lived, however, for within two years of Stanley's humiliating exit from the town, the chiefs did give a piece of ground for a church. Not only that, but they were obliged by native custom to actually help the people to build the church!

3

DELIVERANCE

The early part of Stanley's missionary career was marked by many similar power encounters with the Egbo men. When he returned to Nigeria for his second tour, he was asked to start a school in a new area. Having to set up a school for one hundred and four boys, at four different standards, would have been challenging enough without having to contend with the opposition of witch doctors and the evil powers behind them. His whole passion was that his pupils would come to know the Lord, so much of the teaching was done through the medium of the Scriptures. A large majority of the boys who attended the school did become Christians and some of them went on to serve the Lord as evangelists, so it was not surprising that Stanley met opposition.

Two of those who trusted Jesus came from the Egbo society and their conversion caused great consternation among the pagan chiefs. They determined that they would wreck the school, which had been built in a clearing beside a sacred grove where the Egbo men used to meet.

One evening Stanley and the boys were working in the classroom. The walls had been designed to include an open latticework made from bamboo so that air could circulate freely. As a result, sounds from outside were carried into the room. Stanley was unconcerned when he heard owl calls but he noticed that the boys raised their heads and glanced at each other. He said nothing then, but asked around the next day and discovered that the calls had been made by the Egbo men.

For several nights after that, the strange calls could be heard coming closer and closer to the school building, then fading out as the Egbo men retreated. Stanley could see that the boys were becoming more and more unsettled by the calls and so he decided that something had to be done about it.

The next time he heard the men approaching, lessons had finished for the day and the boys had all gone to bed. Stanley walked over to the dormitories, clapping his hands to announce his arrival, as was the custom.

Immediately all the doors flew open and the boys came rushing out into the moonlit yard.

"What are you doing? Stanley asked. "Were you not asleep?"

"No," they replied, "don't you hear the Egbo men?"

"Yes, I can hear them, but they won't do you any harm."

"Oh yes, they will," one of them said earnestly. "They take sticks and they poke at the mats that cover our windows."

"They want to drop poison into our pots that are along the wall," shouted another and those near him nodded to back up this theory.

"We can't sleep. We're too nervous. We're too afraid of them."

"Listen," said Stanley reassuringly, "the Bible says – there shall no evil befall thee neither shall any harm come nigh thy dwelling. Just go back and pray and lie down and go to sleep again."

The boys took some comfort from the verse of Scripture and gradually lost their fear of the nightly visits. So much so that on one occasion, when the calls came very near and a stick was thrown on to the mat roof of the classroom, the boys jumped up from their seats and announced,

"We're going to go out and catch those men."

"No," said Stanley firmly, "you're not. They are all naked and they're greased with oil. You couldn't catch hold of them but even if you did, they're carrying knives. You're not going out, let's just pray about it."

Stanley read Psalm 90 and the boys somewhat reluctantly went to bed.

The situation was becoming serious but all Stanley could do was to pray and trust that the Lord would undertake. Although he was often very fearful himself, he knew that he couldn't let the boys see that he was afraid, so he used to deliberately leave all the windows of his mud house open. The window of his bedroom was open on to the bush just a few yards behind his house.

One night he prepared for bed as usual, crawled in under his mosquito net, lay down on his bamboo bed and went to sleep. Some time later he woke up with a start and jumped out of bed, wondering what had awakened him so violently. As he stood beside his bed, he felt the room spin round. He thought he was going to faint and he cried out in the name of the Lord, claiming the protection of Jesus' blood. The feeling passed and he lay down again on his bed. Three times that night he was wakened in the same manner but each time he called on the Lord and was able to go back to sleep. He learnt later that the Egbo have a special powder that they can throw into a room to overcome the occupants. He suspected that this was what they were trying to do.

Although he praised God for his own personal deliverance, he was very anxious that God would deliver the boys from the nerve-wracking visits, which had been steadily escalating. The calls were louder, the men were coming closer and their visits were lasting longer and longer. Eventually the boys could take no more and they came to speak to Stanley.

"Etubom, we're going to go home," they said.

Stanley could understand why they felt that way and knew that he was asking a great deal from them when he pleaded with them to stay.

"Let us pray again for one or two more days and see what the Lord may do for us," he suggested. "The government can do nothing for us; the mission can do nothing for us. Let us really count on the Lord to undertake for us. He has promised that no evil shall come near our dwelling."

The boys looked at one another then, one by one, they nodded their assent. Stanley prayed again with them and they went to bed.

He went down to his own little house and began walking up and down the veranda, as he usually did each night, praying.

Suddenly the air was filled with the menacing sound of the hooting. It had begun again. The sounds came nearer and nearer as Stanley prayed to God for deliverance from this evil. As suddenly as it had begun, the noise stopped and was never heard again. Stanley often wondered what had happened – did God send His angels to scare them away? With God, anything is possible.

4

A MISSING MADMAN
and A CRITICAL COLLEAGUE

Not every encounter ended in triumph and Stanley had to come to terms with the fact that sometimes it would prove to be impossible to change the pagan ways of the people. One morning while he was reading his Bible, he heard the most tremendous puffing and blowing and panting down below in the yard. It was very early in the morning but there was light enough to see, so he made his way on to a gangway, which connected the door of the mission station with the kitchen. The kitchen was usually separate from the main part of the house because of the risk of fire. What a sight met his eyes.

Down below was a man, dressed in some very strange garments, holding Stanley's garden fork in his hand. He was holding it like a bayonet, pointing it menacingly at a group of men who were surrounding him.

"What are you doing here?" Stanley shouted.

They all tried to talk at once.

"This is a mad man!............. We had him tied up and he escaped............ He came running into your compound......."

Let us get hold of him again.................He's very dangerous!"

"Oh no", said Stanley, "I'm not going to let you take him."

Now they all looked at Stanley as though he were the madman!

"But he'll kill you" they argued.

Stanley walked down into the yard and began to talk to the man in a calm, quiet voice.

"I'll let you stay here if you will behave yourself and give me the fork."

He wasn't even sure if the man understood what he was saying but he reached out his hand and presented the fork to Stanley. He then meekly followed Stanley to a small downstairs room. Stanley told him to stay there and locked the door.

"Why were you chasing him?" he asked the men who were still standing outside.

"We told you – he is a madman. We had him locked up in his house but he escaped and ran along the road. He had no clothes on so when he came to one of the memorials to the dead, he pulled off some of the cloth that had been draped around it and wrapped it around himself. Then he kept on running until he came to your house."

"Well," thought Stanley, "that explains the strange clothes."

He told the men that they needn't worry any more about the madman as he could stay at Stanley's house.

Next morning while he was having his breakfast, Stanley heard him pacing up and down muttering indistinctly, "lef, right, lef, right, bout turn........." Where he had learnt the military commands no one knew but he spent a lot of his time marching up and down. Stanley and his houseboys fed him and he stayed on their compound for a long time. Then one morning they discovered that he wasn't in his room. They searched all around for him but he was nowhere to be seen. They could only assume that his relatives had come during the night and had taken him away. They never saw him again.

"What do you think would have happened to him," Stanley asked his boys.

"Oh they would take care of him," they replied.

"But how would they do that? How would you take care of someone like that in your village?" he enquired.

The answer shocked and saddened him.

"Well, if we can't beat the madness out of them, then we just tie their feet to a log and starve them and if that doesn't cure them, we would take them out to the forest, tie them to a log and leave them there."

Stanley thought of the heat and the awful thirst and the driver ants and the leopards that roamed in the forest and his heart was filled with sadness at the possible fate of the poor man he had tried to help.

At the beginning of his missionary career he had struggled too with his own personal walk with God. Each morning when he awoke, usually before six o'clock, he took time to be alone with God, his "quiet time". Even at that early hour, many people would already have gathered to speak to the white man, to ask for his help or to hear about the God whom he worshipped. The thought struck him one day that his insistence on having a quiet time before speaking to the people was, in actual fact, selfishness on his part! Surely it would be fairer to deal with the people first and have his quiet time later? So he changed the pattern of his day.

He found, however, that by the time he had finished talking to all his visitors, he was so tired that he needed to rest. Many other things held his attention for the rest of the day and in the cool of the evening, the sick came for medicine. Stanley had no medical training and trying to help them left him just worn out. So it wasn't long before his prayer time was reduced to a weary

"Lord, undertake for me and bless what has been done in your Name, today, and please give me a good night's sleep."

The Lord eventually brought the whole issue to his attention during a visit from a fellow missionary. His colleague, one from whom he would later admit he had not expected to learn anything, took him aside one day and rather shocked him with the observation,

"You know, Stanley, you're greatly changed."

The usually vocal Stanley could only manage a feeble "What?" in reply.

"You're greatly changed since you arrived on the field," his friend repeated.

"How do you mean?" Stanley asked.

"You know, you've got very impatient with the people."

He said no more and during the next few days Stanley became more and more resentful of the criticism.

"Just imagine that man trying to tell me how to behave," Stanley thought. " Imagine him trying to reprove me about such things as that! Doesn't he know the way he lives himself?"

It was no use, of course – he kept hearing the voice of his friend,

"You are very impatient with the people...............You are very impatient with the people.........."

It wasn't very long before the voice of his friend became the voice of God to him and he was honest enough to admit that the criticism was correct. He had been getting all tensed up and he had no patience with anybody. When he asked God why this was happening, the reply came quickly,

"You know why – it's because you've been neglecting your time alone with Me. You don't need to have it while the people are waiting for you downstairs. You can get up and have it before the people begin to come."

Satan had neglected to point out this possibility when he had whispered his lies in Stanley's ear!

5

ANYWHERE EXCEPT ETINAN

Stanley and his new wife, Alice, sat in the large tent and listened intently to the speakers. The grass beneath their feet was uneven, the old church pews on which they were seated were uncomfortable but they returned again and again to the meetings. The Portstewart Convention meetings each June were attended by people from all over Northern Ireland. They enjoyed the fine teaching by well-known speakers, the missionary challenge and the opportunity to meet up with old friends and make new ones.

It was a great joy for Stanley to sit once more under the ministry of the Word in his own language, though he wasn't always totally comfortable with what he heard. God had been challenging him for some time about his willingness to serve in any area where God might choose to send him. So far, his response had always been:

"Yes, Lord, I'm willing to go anywhere in Qua Iboe...........except Etinan."

It's always rather dangerous to put an 'except' clause in to our surrender but Stanley knew that Etinan would prove to be a tough assignment. It was the big central station of the mission and it had run into very bad days. Things had got slack and people were just carrying on as they liked. No one in the mission wanted to be posted to Etinan.

As the week progressed and Stanley listened to the various speakers, he realised that God required complete surrender from him. By the end of the convention, he was able to say,

"By the grace of God, I will go anywhere in Qua Iboe ....even to Etinan."

He and Alice set out for Nigeria on the steamer, using the long sea journey as a part of their honeymoon. When they arrived at Calabar, one of the other missionaries came across the river to meet them and to bring them to their station. He had news for them and was so impatient to tell them that he couldn't even wait until they had disembarked before shouting up to them,

"Stanley, m'boy, you're for it! You're going to Etinan!"

Stanley's calm reaction to the news must have taken the wind out of his sails. God had prepared his heart for this eventuality and he was ready to face the challenge.

Despite the preparation of heart, it wasn't an easy task. They found that things were even worse than they had feared. The elders in one district, a large district that covered about fifty churches, had almost all married more than one wife. What was even worse was that, in an attempt to cover up their wrongdoing, they had an unwritten agreement that anyone who disclosed what was going on, would be put to death! It was not the best way to run a church!

As they talked and prayed about what to do, Stanley remembered some advice he had been given by an older missionary to whom he had been explaining the difficult situation in Etinan.

"I'll tell you what I would do if I were going back to such a situation. I would claim from the Lord two men of the people group to which you would go, who would unreservedly give themselves to God for His service."

This seemed to be very sensible advice, so Alice and Stanley set themselves to pray for two such men. God granted their request and it was a joy to watch two young men, Joseph and Jimmy, grow in grace and faith, realising as they watched that here was God's solution to the problem.

Joseph and Jimmy spent as much time as possible in Stanley and Alice's house. They read the Bible and prayed together and one evening God brought to their attention a verse in 1st John:

"For this cause was the Son of man manifested, that He might destroy the works of the devil."

"Now, Joseph and Jimmy," said Stanley, "do we really believe this? If so, then we must stand on this promise and claim it over all the difficulties we face, over all the irregularities in the Church and everything else. Let us just claim this promise that the victory of the Son of God may be manifested and the devil put to flight."

Their prayer of faith, while delighting the heart of God, aroused the wrath of the evil one and not long after that, Alice and Stanley were wakened up in the night by a tapping noise.

They were living in an old wooden bungalow, which was raised up on pillars, so their bedroom wall was quite high off the ground. The tapping could be heard along the outside wall, beginning at the edge and then coming closer until it seemed to be right behind their pillows.

"What is that?" Alice asked fearfully.

Stanley was anxious to reassure her and said,

"It's just the rats."

"Rats don't make a noise like that," she whispered.

"Well then, let's just ask the Lord about it and remind Him that we are claiming His promise. So if this is of the devil, God will stop it and allow us to get on with our sleep."

They prayed together and God honoured His promise. The tapping stopped and they were able to sleep.

Satan wasn't going to be easily defeated, however.

A few days later, Stanley was walking up and down the veranda, preparing himself for a palaver that was due to take place the following day, claiming this same promise, when the tapping started again.

"Tap, tap, tap," he could hear at the far side of the house. As he continued to pray, he heard it again,

"Tap, tap, tap….."

It was nearer now and seemed to be coming from the ceiling. He tried to ignore it but the tapping continued to creep closer and closer until it was right above his head.

He quickly made his way into the study, where Alice was sitting sewing.

"This tapping has got to stop. If it doesn't it will get us down. Let's pray that if it is of the devil, it will completely stop."

Alice agreed and so the two of them knelt together and claimed that the victory of the Son of God might be manifested in the cessation of the tapping. They were never bothered by it again. Stanley's comment on the situation was simply that it was "not remarkable, of course, because God had done it."

Indeed God did over and above what they had asked for in that district, for not only did they see the resolution of many of the difficulties, but the whole area was blessed by a remarkable visitation of the Holy Spirit in revival. Many came to know Jesus as their Saviour.

Not all the problems he faced were of such grave and serious proportions. On one occasion he was trying to cope with an unsatisfactory houseboy. He soon came to realise, however, that the houseboy was beyond coping with and he would just have to find a new helper. In the end it was all sorted out very easily – his new helper found him!

Stanley and his friend, Bob Taylor, were walking together across the big, open yard of Etinan church one day. They were chatting about various matters, when Stanley noticed a little boy coming towards them. He was about nine years old and small for his age, but he was very neat and clean and strode across the yard in a most business like manner. Stanley stopped to greet him.

"Good morning. What is your name?"

"My name is Samson."

Stanley was amused to hear the tiny little scrap calling himself Samson.

"Tell me, Samson," he asked, "can you read?"

"Yes, sah" he replied.

"And can you read the New Testament in your own language?"

"Yes, sah, and I am baptised," the boy responded.

"Oh then, you love the Lord?"

"Yes, sah."

"Would you like to be a houseboy for me?" Stanley asked. He had been searching for someone to replace the rather unsatisfactory boy and felt that Samson might fit the bill.

"Please, sah, I will go and ask my father, but I would like."

Samson arrived at the school next morning with his father, a stocky, fierce looking man who was one of the local witchdoctors. He was carrying his long witchdoctor's staff.

"You want to see me?" he said.

"Yes," replied Stanley, "I want to know if you will let your son come and live with me. I will put him into school and teach him myself with the other boys and he will live in my house."

The old man looked hard at Stanley for a moment, then he took his son's hand and he took Stanley's hand and he put his son's hand into Stanley's and said,

"He is your son. Take him and train him up aright."

So, next morning, Samson brought his little bundle of belongings and the two of them set off on Stanley's motorbike for Etinan school.

Samson turned out to be a real treasure. He was extremely neat and clean and precise in all he did. He was good at his lessons, eager to learn and a very nice writer, for such a young child. Stanley enjoyed watching him and listening to him as well, for he loved to sing as he worked. It turned out that his native name meant "Song" and Stanley often remarked on how appropriate it was. He seemed to be the perfect houseboy.

After a while, however, Stanley began to suspect that something wasn't quite right. He had porridge every morning for breakfast and a cup of tea with one lump of sugar. He kept a bowl of sugar on the table and noticed that the sugar was going down very quickly for a man who didn't use much. He quickly concluded that Samson had developed a bit of a sweet tooth!

Stanley had his own unique way of dealing with such matters and the next day he called Samson into the study. Samson went to stand beside him and Stanley put his arm around him.

"Tell me," he said gently, "do I give you money for buying your food?"

"Yes, Sah."

"Is it enough?" was the next question.

"Yes."

"And I give you money for your clothes?" Stanley went on.

"Yes, Sah."

"Is it enough?"

"Yes."

"And your soap?"

"Yes, Sah."

"Samson, who does the sugar that you put on the table belong to?" Stanley enquired.

"To you, Sah?" Samson replied, not too sure where this line of questioning was going.

"Samson, listen," Stanley said, looking at the little boy intently, "I want you to tell me the truth. Have you been taking my sugar?"

Samson's head went down and there was a long pause, then he very quietly said,

"Yes, sah."

Stanley gave his shoulder a little squeeze then invited him to kneel beside him and tell the Lord about it.

"You are his child," Stanley reminded him, "and He doesn't want you to take things that don't belong to you. I have plenty of sugar, I know, but it doesn't belong to you and I trust you to look after it."

Samson asked the Lord for forgiveness and from that time on Stanley noticed a change in the young boy. He seemed to have grasped something new about the power of the Lord in his life and was a great witness in the school. In years to come, the simple lesson he learned from Stanley that day would enable him to resist a much greater temptation. He became the Postmaster in a large town and when asked by a friend to lend him money that belonged to the Post office, he knew exactly what his answer had to be.

The church at Etinan grew and often between eight hundred and a thousand people attended the services. Despite the large congregation, the offerings for the Lord's work were very poor, usually amounting to less than two shillings. Stanley felt that it was time the church members were taught about tithing, so he preached a sermon on the subject one Sunday morning.

That afternoon Pastor Joseph arrived to talk to him. "I want to know more about giving a tenth. How do I do it?" he asked.

"Well, Joseph," said Stanley, "supposing you have ten hens and they are all in good condition, giving eggs and having chickens – mark one of them out for God. Then everything that hen produces, you sell and give the money to the Lord."

Joseph nodded in understanding.

"Now make sure you mark one," Stanley continued, "because if you don't and the hawk comes and takes a hen, you will be tempted to say, 'that is God's hen gone'."

Joseph smiled and agreed, recognising that the temptation was indeed very possible.

"Also if you have planted a farm of yams and you have ten mounds of yams, mark one of them as God's mound before it begins to sprout, for the temptation would be if you see a beautiful one sprouting, you will say, 'that one is mine and this one which is not so good is God's'. You will find that the things you mark for God will be well looked after and will do well. So whatever comes into your hand, mark off a tenth of it and give it to God."

Joseph didn't say very much, just looked thoughtful and walked away.

A month later, he called again at the mission house and, after the customary greetings, carefully placed a handkerchief on the table.

"Etubom, I have brought you some money and I want you to please send some of it to different places to help the work of God."

Stanley told him of the work done by such missions as the Sudan United Mission, the China Inland Mission and the Bible Society, inviting him to choose where his tithe should be sent. This little ritual was repeated month by month and the amount of the tithe seemed to grow each month. Then suddenly Joseph stopped bringing the money and Stanley wondered what had happened. Although he saw Joseph on several occasions when they preached together, the subject was never mentioned. Stanley considered that to be between God and Joseph and simply waited to see what would happen.

Many months passed, then Joseph arrived once more with the handkerchief of money and told Stanley what had happened. "This is my money for the Lord," he began. "It's a long time since I have come to give anything. Let me tell you how it is. Some time ago my wife took ill and I had to buy medicine for her. Then my daughter fell ill and I had to buy medicine for her as well. I thought that I just couldn't afford to give any money to the Lord and so I stopped."

"Then, a few days ago, I was going to a palaver in a big church up the country and I wanted to wear my special shirt, the one with the lovely long tail. I went to the box where I kept it and when I opened the box, what did I find? All the clothes in the box had been eaten by white ants. I just stood and stared at it. I couldn't believe my eyes."

"Then I heard God saying to me,

'Joseph, you have been neglecting to give me the tenth which you vowed to give to me, so I had to take it this way.'

This is God's money, not mine. I want you to send it for His work."

So many times Stanley found that he had to teach the new believers very little. God Himself spoke directly into their hearts and guided them into His truth as they learnt to discern His voice.

6

BEHOLD, I SEND AN ANGEL

"Mr Benington," the Chairman said, watching carefully to see Stanley's reaction, "the Qua Iboe Council has been concerned about extending the Mission into new areas where there is no witness."

Stanley gave a little smile as he remembered what he and Alice had talked about on the journey home. He could still see that distant shoreline and could feel the interest rise in his heart again. Having spent some time at home on furlough, he and Alice were beginning to prepare for their return.

"Would you not like to take a trip round into West Africa and see if there is any opportunity for a new work?" the Chairman went on.

"Well, I'm willing to go where I'm sent," was Stanley's reply.

The Chairman gave a little smile.

"And would you ask us to send you then?"

Stanley was polite but forceful.

"No, not on any account, but if you want me to go, I'll go. When I joined the Mission, I was willing to do what was given me to do. I'm still willing to go where I'm sent."

Council spent some time discussing the matter, then made their decision.

"We would like you to go and make a journey through West Africa and report back to the Mission."

Stanley's answer was typical of him,

"I'll have to think about it. If the Lord gives me a word, I will go."

He didn't have to wait long for his word. The very next morning, in his ordinary daily reading, one text stood out:

"Behold, I send an angel before you to lead you in the way and to bring you into the place that I have prepared for you."

That was enough for Stanley.

"Lord," he said, "if that is true, if you have prepared a place for me and You're going to send an angel before me to bring me into the place, then that's O.K. by me."

Council was duly informed and he was given the task of finding out all he could about French West Africa. It proved to be a rather difficult task because very few people knew anything about the area. He did manage to get in touch with the Superintendent of an American mission, the Christian Missionary Alliance. Their headquarters was in French Guinea, which was on the western side of French West Africa, just south of Senegal. He assured Stanley that there was plenty of room in the area for any number of missions.

"Do come along," he said, "there's lots of space and you will find some roads. Bring a car and you can follow the main roads."

The more Stanley thought about the great adventure that now lay before him, the more excited he became. He was thrilled by the idea of exploring new territory, facing new challenges and meeting new people. He was delighted at the prospect of introducing Jesus to people groups who had never heard of Him.

He understood, of course, the nature of the task he was under-taking and the dangers he would face. He knew that he might well encounter wild animals, bush fires, impassable roads, impenetrable jungle and maybe even savage cannibals but he also knew that he could rely on God for protection and guidance.

There was just one cloud on the horizon – the journey he was about to undertake was totally unsuitable for Alice and their little boy, Russell. His heart was heavy as he thought of leaving them behind but when he and Alice discussed the matter, they both realised that there was no other possibility. Although they could have accompanied him to Nigeria and lived on one of the missionary compounds there while Stanley headed into this new uncharted territory, in the end they both agreed that the most sensible thing to do was to stay in Ireland until Stanley could establish a home for them. Where that would be, of course, they had no idea. All Stanley knew was that God had promised "a place prepared" and an angel to guide him there and that was enough for him.

Alice too had proved God to be utterly faithful in the previous years in Nigeria and she was prepared to take God at His word, depending on Him to protect her husband as he journeyed into the unknown. She had peace in her heart and a confidence that God would fulfil His promise. That didn't stop her dreading the parting or the lonely months without Stanley, but it did bring comfort and strength.

So the two of them worked together, planning Stanley's trip. They talked about it, they prayed about it, they bought supplies for it and they told their supporters about it. Stanley's well-being and safety would be at risk and he might well encounter difficulties they could not anticipate, so it was vitally important that their prayer partners should be well informed and encouraged to pray earnestly for him.

In August 1930, Stanley spent some time in France, improving his knowledge of the French language, before setting sail for Nigeria in November. Soon after his arrival, he had the opportunity to speak to the Church Conference of Qua Iboe. He told them of the Council's desire to extend the work to areas where Jesus was not known and gave them some information about French West Africa. His words filled his listeners with amazement and the oldest pastor, Pastor Joseph, spoke for all of them when he addressed the gathering.

"We have heard with wonder what you have been telling us. We thought that the Gospel had been to every part of the world and then came to the last place, to the last people who had not heard. We didn't know that there were still people who had not heard of the Lord."

There was a murmur of assent from those around him and heads nodded gravely as his fellow pastors took in this information.

"How much money have we got in our funds?" he asked the treasurer.

"We have £200," was the reply.

"Well, I propose," Pastor Joseph said, "that this £200 be given to Etubom Benington to go out and do this work and we will get more money for what we need."

Stanley was greatly pleased with their gift, not just because of its practical use, but because it was an indication of the Church's desire to be involved in missionary enterprise. Stanley recognised this desire to see the Gospel, which they had embraced with such enthusiasm, brought to people in other countries as an important step forward in the development of the Qua Iboe Church.

This desire was not limited to the pastors and church leaders. One old lady, who had been the first woman convert in Qua Iboe, was most interested in the story of Stanley's journey and felt compelled to bring a gift to Mrs Bill, the wife of Samuel Bill, the founder of the mission. Her story touched Gracie Bill so much that she reported it in the next mission magazine:

"Old Etia is fairly well but very frail. Although troubled by illness at night, she can visit sick folk during the day. She was in here at 8a. m. after attending the early morning prayer meeting and visiting a woman. Her prayers are wonderful. She just lives with Jesus and prayer is her very breath.

She is very interested in Mr Benington's journey in French Africa and in the new country up the Niger. Some of the missionaries had been here and had given her five shillings. She brought it to me with twenty-one threepenny bits wrapped up in paper. She had been gathering these for a long time and had them hidden under a box. She handed me the ten shillings and three pence, the first contribution from this part of Qua Iboe towards the new work.

Poor old dear, she feels she can never love the Lord enough."

7

13,000 MILES IN A MODEL T

By 26th January 1931, all the final preparations had been made. Stanley had bought a Ford car, a Model T, and had got it fitted up with extra boxes. He sold some of his possessions and used the money to buy supplies for the journey. One of his former house boys, called Kano, agreed to go with him and the two of them set out with a great sense of excitement and a prayer in their hearts that God would keep them following the promised angel. Stanley felt like Abraham going into Canaan or Paul going into Greece!

Their first destination was Lagos, the Nigerian capital, where they managed to get a passport for his houseboy, Kano and permission to leave the country. They then drove through the length of Nigeria, into Niger, where they crossed the River Niger at Niamey, on 18th February. Their journey then took them to Fada-n-Gourma, which was near the eastern border of Upper Volta, (now known as Burkina Faso), right across Upper Volta and eventually on to Kankan in French Guinea.

As they drove through French West Africa, they came across unreached people groups every day. Although his sense of adventure exulted in the new sights and sounds all around him, his heart was saddened as he drove through village after village where the gospel had not yet penetrated. His report home reflected this sadness:

"The Need.

As I write that word, my heart goes up in a great cry. The need is awful, both in magnitude and urgency. I cannot describe it and I cannot hope to impart to others any idea of the vastness of the countries and populations I have seen utterly without the Gospel."

Kankan was the centre of the Christian and Missionary Alliance Work and it was there they met Mr Roseberry, the Field Super-intendent. He gave them lots of information about the people groups in the area and made various suggestions regarding places where they could begin to work, but Stanley refused to be drawn into making any decision. He still had many miles to travel and as yet God had given him no indication of the place where he should work. So he and Kano set out once again in the little Ford car, driving on across to the western coast of Africa and around Senegal, passing the long, weary miles by chatting together, when the rough roads allowed conversation. Since Kano couldn't speak either French or English, their conversation was conducted in Kano's native tongue.

As they passed through Senegal, they came to an area in the south of the country where at first they had thought there were no missionaries but then had discovered that two people were working in the lower Casamance for the Christian Missionary Alliance.

"Maybe we should make a detour and go and see them," Stanley had suggested to the Chairman of the mission, who had told him about them.

The Chairman had been delighted with this plan.

"That would be grand," he had assured Stanley. "They are all alone there, thousands of miles away from us. They have no fellowship at all and it would be lovely if you called."

About five miles from their house they came to a river that had no bridge across it. Kano looked at Stanley and wondered just how this crazy white man was going to solve this problem – it seemed insurmountable to him! He watched in astonishment as Stanley, using a mixture of broken French and frantic sign language, managed to arrange for two canoes to be tied together and brought close to the bank of the river. Surely he wasn't going to attempt to put the car on the canoes?

He held his breath as Stanley carefully manoeuvred the little Ford car until it was perched on the canoes. As they slowly crossed the river, Stanley explained that he had done this many times before. It was risky but it worked.

By this time, evening was approaching and Stanley was feeling hot and sticky after his exertions with the canoes and the car. Suddenly even the muddy water of an African river seemed inviting.

"What about a dip?" he asked Kano.

Soon the two of them had stripped off and were splashing around in the cool water. Never had a bathe seemed so wonderful!

It was getting dark as they approached the thatched mud house that was the mission station. The tall South African missionary and his little Dutch wife came running out when they heard the toot of the horn. The missionary would later admit,

"When I saw that white leg with nothing but a gym shoe on the end of it, I thought to myself, 'My, what are we coming to?'"

The reason for his consternation was that all the other expatriates wore long trousers, despite the intense heat, because that was the French custom. Stanley didn't realise it at the time, but he would be held responsible for introducing shorts to that part of the country!

At dinner that evening, Stanley was congratulating the other couple on their location.

"You know, you're lucky having that river so near to you," he said. "You can pop in for a bathe anytime."

"Did you bathe there?" the missionary asked.

"Rather," Stanley replied enthusiastically. "It had been such a fearfully hot day and we just revelled in it."

"Well, I'm glad to see you here in one piece." The missionary told him. "That river is infested with crocodiles. Nobody bathes there!"

Now that the danger was over, Stanley's sense of humour came into operation.

"Well," he laughed, "any decent crocodile, seeing me, would know there was no meat to spare!"

There would be even less meat to spare by the end of the long journey, for Stanley lost over three stone as a result of the limited diet he was forced to eat. He had brought some tinned food but it soon ran out and for the last part of the journey, his diet consisted mainly of rice with the few extras he could find in the village markets. So the meals they shared with the two missionaries during their few days' stay in the remote mission station were doubly welcome.

During one of their chats, Stanley's new found friend suggested that they should visit a particular area but Stanley was reluctant to do so because neither he nor Kano could speak the local dialect.

"Oh don't let that stop you," came the reply, "I'll lend you a chap to go with you."

So Marmadu joined the expedition for a while, travelling with them into the nearby forest areas, where Paganism and Islam existed side by side. Many of those who had converted to Islam retained their pagan practices, continuing to worship idols and make sacrifices to them.

The two boys, one a Muslim and one a Christian, lived together for ten days, sleeping on the same mat at night, sometimes under the car, sometimes under the stars, sometimes in the back room of a rest house, sometimes in the same room as Stanley. Every morning Kano had his prayer time and read his Efik New Testament and Marmadu watched all that went on but they had no language in common so they had no way of talking about God together.

Stanley brought him back to his mission station at the end of the trip, then he and Kano headed off again, around the north part of Senegal and then on along the southern edge of the Sahara Desert, towards Timbucktou, in Mali. They wondered if they would ever hear of the missionary couple or Marmadu again.

Right in the heart of Senegal, the little Ford car got stuck in the sand one night. Stanley knew that they were near the provincial capital of the area but he also knew that the people were strongly Muslim, so he wondered what sort of reception he would get if he went for help. Much to his surprise, the chief insisted that his men should help him to manhandle the car out of the sand and insisted that Stanley should spend the night in a nearby resthouse. He then sent along his assistant, who could speak French, to help Stanley and Kano settle in for the night. They chatted as they worked and Stanley discovered that, despite being a Muslim, the man's heart was hungry to hear about Jesus. They talked for some time and then the man left, clutching the little Gospel that Stanley had given to him.

He came back early the next morning and, from the long conversation they had, Stanley guessed that he had spent most of the night reading the Gospel. Stanley took great delight in explaining just how a man could receive new life from God and the power to live a life of victory over sin. He never heard from him again but Stanley was content that he had shared God's word and that God had promised it would not return to Him empty.

Although he never knew how that particular encounter ended, he did hear some very encouraging news about another young man whose life he had impacted on this amazing journey.

One year later, in another part of French West Africa, hundreds of miles away from the mission station where he had first met him, Stanley met up with his South African missionary friend once more.

"You know, Stanley," he said, "a wonderful thing happened just a month ago."

"What was that?" Stanley asked.

"You remember the boy I lent you, to take you around?"

"Yes," Stanley said, "Marmadu, wasn't it?"

"That's right, Marmadu. At the last baptismal service, Marmadu was baptised."

Stanley was delighted to hear this news.

"There were several baptised together," his friend went on, "and that night we lit a camp fire. We sat around it chatting, and I began to ask what had brought them to the Lord, thinking that perhaps one of my sermons had been responsible! Marmadu's answer was a great surprise.

'Actually, it wasn't any sermon at all,' he said. 'Do you remember that last year a white man came round here and he brought his Nigerian boy with him and I went off with them for ten days?'

'Well, I lived with them in the motor for all that time. That boy and I slept together, ate together, bathed together, travelled together and I watched him and I saw him reading a book every morning and I saw him praying. Well I watched him carefully and he never stole anything belonging to his master and he never deceived his master. I said to myself that there must be something in that book that I don't know about, so when I went back to the mission station, I began to go to the services and I learned to read and I found out what he had. He had the Lord Jesus Christ in his heart as his Saviour and that is the reason why I have come to Him and why I have been baptised.'"

"What a splendid story," said Stanley, "and it just proves what I have always believed, that people can be won for the Lord by a good walk before them."

Six long, hot months and 13,000 long dusty miles later, Stanley and Kano drove into the headquarters of the American mission where they had begun their journey. They had survived the humidity of the jungle, they had traversed semi-desert roads choked by Sahara sands and water-logged flats intersected by creeks and their hearts were full of praise to the great God who had watched over them, guiding them and protecting them every step of the way.

8

THE PLACE PREPARED

Stanley knelt by his bed in the C.M.A. mission headquarters in Kankan, gazing intently at the large map spread out in front of him. Where would God have him go? To which people group was he to take the Gospel? He had passed through so many needy places, he had seen so many needy people. He couldn't go to all of them. He had to make a choice. Should he take the Gospel to a pagan people group, or to a Muslim group? How could he possibly choose? He had to know the mind of God, so he prayed earnestly that God would clearly reveal His will. He was particularly drawn to the Gouransi people group, largely because they seemed to be ready to receive the Gospel.

As well as praying for guidance, he spent some time writing a report for the mission and requested that they would tell him whether to start work in the west among the Islamic people or in the east among the pagan people. Their answer would narrow the possibilities for him, so he awaited their cable with some excitement. When the cable came it said quite simply, "Establish east."

The Gouransi people group was in the east and Stanley was rather excited at the prospect of beginning a work among them, but the more he prayed about it, the more the Lord seemed to be telling him to go to the Lobi people group. Stanley knew very little about the Lobis except that they had a fearsome reputation as the most wicked people in West Africa. They were known as the Robbers of West Africa.

Each time he took out the map to pray over it, the Lobis came into his mind so eventually he had a look at the area in which they lived. He saw a name marked on the map – Bouroum-Bouroum and the Lord said to him,

"You'll find the place near that."

The loads were soon repacked and arrangements made for the move into Lobi land and in all the busyness of those days the name Bouroum-Bouroum was forgotten, though Stanley was clear about the area to which he was now sure God had called him.

He first of all made contact with Mr. Roseberry, the head of the Christian Missionary Alliance. He met up with him at a conference where Stanley was asked to address the missionaries. While he was there, he met a little Lobi boy who had become a Christian as a result of attending a Bible class. Stanley discovered that this little boy had been praying for a year that God would send a man to tell his people about Jesus. What a joy it was to be the answer to his prayer.

"We're going to establish among the Lobi people, " Stanley told Mr. Roseberry, "we feel the Lord is leading us there."

"That's grand," was the enthusiastic reply, "we've heard a lot about them but we have no men to send to the area so we're very glad that you're able to go."

"But," he added, "you're not thinking of going in now?"

"Oh yes," Stanley assured him, "we're going as soon as possible."

"Well now," Mr. Roseberry warned him, "this is the beginning of the wet season – you won't be able to build a house in the wet season."

"That's not a problem – we'll find a house there."

Mr. Roseberry shook his head.

"Oh no, you won't," he said. "You won't find a house in the Lobi country because they are a very peculiar people – they live in mud houses, built without any windows like caves under the earth. This keeps them cool in the intense heat but it also means that they are very dark."

But nothing he could say would quench Stanley's conviction that the place and the timing were right.

"Well," he said, "we'll find a house."

"And will there be curtains in the windows?" teased Mr. Roseberry.

"Yes, there'll be curtains at the windows!"

"And geraniums?"

"No," laughed Stanley, "there'll be no geraniums."

Soon Stanley and his houseboy were on their way, staying in Government resthouses, which were to be found every 40 or 50 miles along the road. They weren't pleasant places to stay but they had brought camp beds with them so at least they had somewhere clean to sleep.

They travelled over 1500 miles round into the Lobi people group, coming into the area from the north, along a track through the forest. Sure enough, they saw round Lobi mud houses on every hand, scattered about randomly, each one surrounded by its own farmland. There seemed to be no villages and, as far as they could see, nowhere for them to stay.

Suddenly, Stanley's boy shouted out,

"Etuboum, there's a house! Up there – through that cutting in the forest."

Stanley stopped and then backed the car. Through the trees, about a quarter of a mile away, he could see a square house. It had obviously been built for a European because it was square and had curtains at the windows!

"No geraniums," Stanley thought impishly, before a more serious thought struck him –

"Maybe this is the prepared place."

Together they swept out the little house, set up their camp beds and Stanley went right to work. He noticed a man coming towards him – he had a bow over his shoulder and was carrying a quiver of arrows on his arm. The man put up his right hand to show that there was nothing in it, indicating that he meant Stanley no harm, and said, "Min fuor fer". Stanley wrote down what he had heard and waited for someone else to pass by.

Soon another man arrived and Stanley quickly put up his hand before the man could and tried out the word he had learnt.

"Min fuor fer".

"Min fuor fer acha," the man replied, so now Stanley knew one of the greetings and its reply. In that way, by the end of the first evening in Lobi land, he had recorded between 20 and 30 phrases.

Next morning they visited the French Commander, who was rather cross that they had stayed in the house they had found in Bomoi without his permission. He had been the Military Governor of Madagascar but had been brought in to administer affairs among the Lobis because they were such a war-like people and the French Government needed someone who could handle them. Stanley explained that they had come to do mission work, to give the people the Word of God.

"Well, you can't stay there," he said.

"Why is that?" asked Stanley.

"That area is a very dangerous corner of the Lobi territory. You are British and you would be very close to the British border of the Gold Coast. If anything happened to you, there would be trouble."

Stanley wasn't put off at all by the thought of trouble, so he asked if they could apply to the Governor.

"Yes, certainly," came the reply, "you can send an application and I will sign it for you in a favourable way."

Despite his stern exterior, the commander proved to be a real help, making out their papers in the official French that was required for the documents. Stanley hoped that they had indeed found the "prepared place" but it wasn't to be – the Governor refused their application. It turned out that the house they had spotted in the forest had been built for some former Catholic missionaries but the Lobis had taken a dislike to them and had put them out.

Stanley decided to go to visit the Governor himself – perhaps his Irish charm might work where all else had failed! The Governor was extremely pleasant, a very friendly man, but he was not prepared to change his mind. He was happy enough for them to settle amongst the Lobis but not in that particular village.

"And you will have to be very careful in the way you behave," he added, "because the striking of a match could put the whole people group up in flames. However, I wish you every success in your work in future years."

Stanley felt rather discouraged by all of this but he went back to the local commander who gave them permission to stay in one of the rest houses while he built his house in the safer area. The next morning he and his houseboy set out northwards along the main track. About forty kilometres further on, they came to a rest house and stopped to take a look. It was really more like a compound, with a big hut in the centre and four huts around it.

"What do you think about this one?" Stanley asked his companion.

"Shall we go on to the next one and take a look at it?" was the reply.

Stanley nodded his agreement and they made their way on up the track to another rest house.

"Well, what do you think of this one?" Stanley asked.

"I think the first one was better," the boy answered.

"So do I," agreed Stanley.

They had permission to stay in the rest house as long as they needed to, so Stanley and his boy soon settled in. It wasn't long before he found out the name of the village where he had chosen to settle – it was Bouroum-Bouroum. Suddenly it all came back to him – the map laid out on the bed and the voice that had whispered in his ear,

"You'll find the place near that."

The angel who led the way had made no mistakes. They had come to the place prepared for them!

9

PATIENCE....PATIENCE

There were about 80,000 Lobis in Upper Volta. They were a hardworking people, farming maize, millet and bean crops. The women sowed the seed and the men did all the heavy labour, rising early to start work in the fields at 5 a.m., resting for an hour or two in the middle of the day and then working until sunset.

They were also great fighters and before the French Government introduced their ideas about law and order, most quarrels had been sorted out with the help of bows and barbed arrows. The women liked to have little discs of wood inserted in their lips and the men were proud of their coloured beads and the glossy shine that vegetable oil gave to their skin.

Stanley was eager to get to work – a house had to be built and a language had to be learnt. The second would prove to be more difficult than the first. He tried his best to get friendly with the people but the Lobis just wouldn't be friendly. The men stood at the doors of their houses, with their bows and arrows all ready and the women wouldn't even come out! But Stanley wasn't one to give up easily and despite the fact that he couldn't converse with them at all, they seemed to recognise that he meant them no harm and allowed him to listen and watch as they farmed and hunted.

He often wondered about the promise he had been given and the conviction he still held that he had been led to a prepared place. Surely, he reasoned, God wouldn't have sent him to a prepared place unless He had a prepared people too. Until he learned the language, he had no way of knowing if the people had been prepared or not, so he struggled on, listening to the rhythms of the language and writing it down as accurately as possible. He remembered the words of the professor in Switzerland who had tried to help him learn the French language,

"Don't mind if you don't hear anything. Just sit and listen and get the music of the language in your ear."

Gradually he began to understand and even to communicate.

It was a lonely life without his much-loved wife and little son, Russell. Plans had been made for them to join him - the helpful French Commandant had arranged that the postal van which brought his own mail down from the large town, 150 miles away, should stop at Stanley's door to deliver and collect mail so he and Alice had been able to communicate in this way. Until that time, however, he was forced to manage on his own. It wasn't easy and this was reflected in one of his letters home:

"It is difficult to live day after day, struggling with the language of a heathen people, watching their lives and being watched, seeing and hearing little good and much evil, without the help of congenial company of any kind, without feeling isolation and depression. Add to this, living in dark, comfortless quarters and the impossibility of making real friendship with anyone."

Day after day, he listened intently to everything that was said by those around him, writing it all down in his notebook in the phonetic alphabet. He had found that the best way to learn a language was to learn phrases rather than single words and try to work out how the phrases changed in different contexts. Once he had managed to learn a few phrases, he was able to interact a little with the young boys who would congregate near his house to see this strange white man and his equally strange mode of transport. Stanley had brought a bicycle with him – the first bicycle to be seen in that area – and it proved to be a great attraction.

The boys were soon at ease with him and allowed him to go hunting with them. Eventually Stanley had enough little phrases to translate a few texts of scripture and he taught these to the boys. One of them was the verse, "He who hath the Son hath life: he who hath not the Son hath not life,"

It didn't matter to him that he couldn't explain what the verses meant. He simply believed that God's Word wouldn't return to Him empty. Nearly twenty years later, when he returned to the area after a long absence, he met one of the men to whom he had taught the verses.

"He who hath.." Stanley began.

".....the Son hath life," the man finished the text with a twinkle in his eye. God's Word had been firmly lodged in his heart and mind.

In December Stanley made the long journey to Grand Bassam on the Ivory Coast to meet Alice and his little boy. He brought them to the Christian Missionary Alliance Headquarters, where they stayed while he took the heavy loads through into Lobi land. He then went back for them and in February 1932, brought them to the newly finished house in Bouroum-Bouroum. It was a simple structure of dried mud blocks and a grass roof. The walls were about two feet deep and the grass thatch was laid on thickly and extended beyond the walls to create a shady verandah. It had no ceilings inside and no proper windows or doors, just holes in the walls. It was designed in this way to ensure that the interior would be as cool as possible.

They soon settled in and Alice brought her own womanly touches to the mud house and it gradually began to feel more like home. The compound rang to the shouts of "Dada" as little Russell followed Stanley about. The Lobis thought this was his name and began to call Stanley "Daouda", the closest they could get to the English sounds.

Soon after her arrival, Alice realised that she was pregnant and they thanked God for the gift of another child, praying that Alice would keep healthy and that the baby would be delivered safely.

While down at the coast, Stanley had engaged the services of two men, a mason and a cook, called Koulemba. The cook had been a Muslim, but the missionaries thought that he had become a

Christian. Although Koulemba couldn't speak much French, Stanley and he were able to converse quite well on the long journey to Bouroum-Bouroum and back again. He seemed a pleasant boy and was very helpful around the house. He learnt to speak Lobi before Stanley did and he used to attend the little services that Stanley began to hold, on the verandah of the house, for his family and those who worked for him on the compound.

Koulemba helped Alice with the cooking and the washing and other household chores but gradually they noticed that he was discontented. Stanley felt that he was deliberately doing things to annoy Alice and after watching this go on for a while, he could stand it no longer.

"Dear, let's send Koulemba home," he suggested. "He really is too exasperating for words."

"Well," replied Alice, "you know we are praying for him and it would be nice if we had patience and tried him a little longer."

"It's up to you," Stanley said, "you have to work with him but really and truly it's not fair the way he treats you and the way he does things."

Alice nodded in agreement.

"I know, but just let's have patience and try and keep on praying for him."

So Koulemba stayed and Alice patiently put up with his awkward little ways.

The mason had already been interested in the Gospel, so Stanley started to do language study with him, using the Gospel of John. As a result of the study, the mason accepted Christ as his Saviour.

A third member of the tiny congregation on the verandah was Dakona, the new gardener. He had been a soldier with the French so he could read French well and after a while he began to read the New Testament in French. His wife asked him why he was always reading "that book".

"Ah," he replied, "this is something that is really good. I would be very content to take this Master into my heart."

Some time later he knelt with Stanley and prayed in French for the pardon of his sins. He thanked the Lord for dying for him and asked Him to take up His home in his heart.

Much as these conversions thrilled Stanley, he was still impatient for the time when the first Lobi would turn from his idols to serve the true and living God. First of all, he had to learn enough of the language, so it was back to the pencil and notebook, listening and writing……….. listening and writing.

10

BREAKTHROUGH

One of the limitations placed on Stanley by the French Governor was that he must not preach the Gospel outside his house. He could preach inside as much as he liked, but the problem was that even when he had acquired enough of the Lobi language to begin preaching, he couldn't get the Lobis to come to his house. He and Alice prayed about the problem and waited to see how God would resolve the situation.

At the end of the dry season that year, early in July, the rains began. At first they were good, drenching the dry, caked soil with much-needed water and the crops began to grow. The maize, millet, yams and sweet potatoes were in good condition.

Then the rains ceased. The skies were cloudless and the sun beat down relentlessly. As the ground became drier and drier, the crops began to suffer. They were already about four feet high, just coming into fruition and they really needed the rain. As the days went by, the people began to get anxious.

The chief of the district made his way to the Benington house.
"Daouda," Chief Shintete asked, "are you stopping the rain?"
"No," Stanley replied, "I'm not stopping the rain."
"Well," the old man went on, "the crops are dying. They need rain."
"You want rain?" questioned Stanley.
"Yes," was the emphatic reply.
"Well, bring the headmen of the village in here tomorrow and I'll tell you how to get rain."

Much prayer rose to Heaven that night from the little mud house in Bouroum-Bouroum, prayer that God would use this opportunity to glorify His Name among the Lobi people.

Next day, about forty or fifty men filed on to the verandah –they carried their bows and arrows and axes over their shoulders. They listened intently as Stanley explained the Gospel as clearly as he could. With Dakona's help, he told them that if they would pray to God, in the Name of His Son, and destroy their idols, He would send the rain.

When he had finished speaking, an old man said that they had heard and were glad that the Word of God had come to them.

"But," he went on, "we would like to be sure that it was true. We don't know your God, but you do. So, if you pray to Him and He sends rain, we will believe."

"Well now," thought Stanley, "that's a fair challenge."

With a hurried but earnest prayer to God in Heaven, Stanley accepted the challenge.

"O.K. I'll pray for rain."

The men left and this modern-day Elijah fell on his face to plead with God for rain. He thought to himself,

'Now this is great. I'll pray and just go outside and look at the sky and see a cloud just as big as a man's hand coming and the people will think that this man really knows God and knows the way to get things from God.'

He wasn't to know that God had a different plan, one that would bring the glory to Him and not to Stanley Benington.

"God in Heaven," he prayed, " You know how important this is. If the rain doesn't come, I might as well pack my bags and go home because the people won't believe anything I say."

"Now," he sensed God say to him, "you just leave the rain to Me and you pray for what I sent you here for – that these people might be brought to a knowledge of the Lord Jesus Christ."

A week went by and no rain had fallen. Every time Stanley and Alice went out, they saw the seared crops and the people standing at their doors or walking through the millet fields, wondering if anything would be left. Chief Shintete came back with the same plea – the crops were dying and needed rain.

"When will the rain come?" he asked.

"Bring the people in here again tomorrow," Stanley said.

At the service next day, Dakona, the gardener, spoke on the verse, "you must be born again", and asked for questions at the end. The village butcher went forward and said that the people believed that Jesus was God's Son. They had been thinking about Him and had stopped making sacrifices. Each night as they went to bed, they thought that perhaps before morning the Son of God would give them rain, but the rain did not come.

"What shall we do for food?" he went on. "Much of the maize is dead. But if Christ sends rain either today or tomorrow, we will know that He is indeed the Son of God."

Stanley assured them that he would pray to that end and the men left once more.

All that week Stanley and Alice prayed and watched the sky for clouds and listened for the sound of distant thunder but there was nothing. They prayed and waited and never lost the assurance that God heard their cries.

The people came again on Sunday. Once again Stanley told them that they had to turn from their idols and worship the true God, once again the men listened intently but this time there were no questions at the end, only a stony silence.

By Wednesday, Chief Shintete was very distressed.

"Daouda, the crops are dead and the rain is not coming," he said sadly.

"Are they really dead?" Stanley asked.

"No," the chief said, "but they will only last for another day or two."

"Then, when a day or two is past, bring the people back again."

That evening, while Stanley and Dakona were reading the Bible together, a little rain began to fall, only just enough to keep the remaining stalks alive. For the next three days there were plenty of clouds in the sky but very little rain.

On Sunday, 7th August, the people came once more to the verandah. They listened even more intently and at the end, Stanley said to them,

"Now is there anybody here – anybody who would like to accept the Son of God as Saviour and destroy his idols?"

Two men stood up and indicated that they would, so Stanley asked the others to go and the two men to remain behind.

"Did you understand what I said?" Stanley asked them.

"Yes, " they nodded, "and we would like to accept the Son of God as Saviour."

So they knelt together on the verandah and Stanley went over it all again, just to be sure they really understood what they were doing. Then they both asked the Son of God to come into their hearts, wash their hearts clean in His blood, live in their hearts and give them power to live a new life. The two men got to their feet.

"Now," said Stanley, "you must go home and destroy your idols."

The men looked at each other and then at Stanley.

"Oh, we don't have any idols."

"You must have," Stanley insisted. "I've been round your village many times and there are idols everywhere – in your houses, outside on your roof, beside the rivers, in your farms."

One of them then told him a story that amazed him.

"Ten or eleven years ago, God spoke to me. I was going to be made a witch doctor. I was going to be raised in rank as a full witch doctor. The sacrifices had all been collected, my wives had made the beer. Everything was ready. The chiefs were coming in the morning and the witch doctors from all around were coming for the celebrations and the initiation ceremony."

"That night, as I lay asleep," he went on, "God came and pushed me over the side of the roof, where I was sleeping. He did that three times. Then he spoke to me and called me by name.

'Tigite,' His voice said, 'destroy your idols. The day for sacrificing to idols has passed. I am going to send a white man and his wife into your village to tell you My way.'

I got up in the morning early and I began to destroy my idols."

"Of course, the idols were not only mine, but also my family's and as soon as the people heard the noise, my father rushed out. He was the headman of our village at that time and he grabbed me, calling to my brothers and the other people in the house to come and catch me, shouting that I had gone mad."

"About twenty or thirty people came running out after me. They caught me, bound me and threw me into the bush. That was what usually happened if anyone destroyed an idol. I lay in the bush, helpless and thought that I would die. Night fell and then I heard someone creeping quietly towards me. It was one of the old women of the village. She cut my bonds and set me free."

"From then on, I went around the village and other villages nearby, telling the people that God had sent a message to them to destroy their idols and hundreds of people destroyed their idols. We used to meet together and sing together and eat together, all those of us who believed that God was going to send a man with His message."

"Then," he continued, "the people got tired and accused me of destroying our customs. The chiefs of the people group took me to the French Governor at Ouagadougou, about four hundred miles away, to complain that I was destroying their customs and that the whole people group would rise up against me. The Governor heard my story and wrote me out a paper saying that I could continue to preach and no one was to molest me."

Stanley wondered if it was the same Governor who had been so helpful to him, but was assured that it had been a previous Governor, a man who professed to be an atheist! Tigite continued with his story, his face downcast as he told what had happened.

"I went back and continued to preach but a year passed and no white men came. Two years passed, three.... four.... five years and the people began to take their idols back again. They had no one to help them, no one to guard them, no one to protect them, no one to go to when they were sick. What were they to do? They had to take their idols back again."

"But," he went on, "I believed what God had told me and I continued to live without idols. So we have no idols to burn."

"Well, that's grand," said Stanley, delightedly, amazed at the faithfulness of these two men who had patiently waited for so many years.

"We do have three things," added Tigite. "When God told me to preach His message around the people group, He said not to take bows and arrows, but to take a sword, light bulbs and a blood red flag. The flag I used to display outside my house so that when people asked what it was, I would tell them that I had obeyed God by destroying my idols."

Stanley thought of all the Christian symbolism inherent in those three items and marvelled at the way God had brought a measure of enlightenment to these people, before any missionary had even set foot in their land. He thought too of the significance of the words - "a white man and his wife". There had been few white men living in that part of West Africa at the time and even fewer brought their wives to stay with them. The prophecy given to Tigite had been fulfilled in every detail.

Stanley also wondered for a moment why they had to wait eleven years for the promised messenger. Why did he have to leave Qua Iboe, where he really knew the language and was enjoying the work? Why did he have to make the journey when any young man could have done it? Had someone been disobedient to the voice of God, or was it all just part of the mysterious dealings of God with mankind? Of course, he reasoned, God's purposes cannot be frustrated entirely – He does His will in the army of the heavens and among the inhabitants of the earth eventually. Anyway, a God whose every action he could understand wouldn't be God and wouldn't be worth worshipping. Whatever the reason, his heart was full of thanksgiving to the God who had allowed him to hear the story and sent His angel to lead him to the very village where Tigite and his friend lived.

The men went back to their huts and that very evening, Stanley was standing looking out over the country towards the South West and he saw the clouds beginning to form. The sky grew darker, the wind rose and shook the trees all around, the lightning flashed on and off, lighting up the whole sky and the thunder rumbled endlessly, increasing in volume and intensity, until, with an almighty crack, the storm broke and the long awaited rain fell at last. No gentle rain this time, but a prolonged, penetrating rain that reached deep into the parched soil.

As he dashed around the house, checking the all the water barrels were in place, his heart was singing a song of praise to the One who had so spectacularly answered his prayer.

Next day, Chief Shintete was back again.

"Now we know," he said, "that the rain came from God."

"How do you know?" asked Stanley.

The chief pointed to the nearest farm.

"Even the crops that were dead are living again."

Stanley realised that the dead crops coming back to life would have great significance for the Lobi people because death and death ceremonies were what preoccupied them more than anything else. So he began to understand to some extent why they had to wait for so many weeks for God to show forth His power. God wanted to demonstrate to these people that not only could He send rain, but He could also bring back to life that which had been dead.

Before he went to sleep that night, Stanley wrote home to those who partnered him in the Gospel,

"We thank you for the way you have been upholding us. We plead for real labour in prayer for those who have taken the Lord and then for those who are still hesitating. Shintete and an old soldier are both near the kingdom.

This has been written under a real sense of the goodness of God and with a deep joy and wonder at what God has wrought. Isn't it wonderful that we have settled down in the very town where this man has been waiting for the Word for eleven years?"

Some time later, on 30th September, the Beningtons had further cause to rejoice when Alice was safely delivered of a baby girl in the hospital at Ouagadougou. They named her June.

The meetings on the verandah continued and in the months that followed, word spread to other villages about the white man's teaching. One Sunday morning in January, a tall, thin, old man arrived and waited for the service to begin. He was followed not long afterwards by the chief of his village. Stanley got into conversation with the two men and discovered that they came from Banlo, a village a few miles away, and that the witchdoctor had already stopped worshipping his idols. He was quite clear that he had sinned and wished to receive the Son of God into his heart. They knelt down, there and then, and the witchdoctor gave his life to the Lord. When questioned, the chief said that he wanted to know God's way but added that he had never done anything wrong. They invited him to the services and, after the evening service, he talked at length with Stanley's cook, who convinced him of his sin, and he too accepted Christ.

This was the beginning of a movement of God in Banlo. In his report home, Stanley recorded what happened:

"Then the others requested me to come to the village early next morning, as people were desirous of destroying their idols. I was on the road long before dawn, and found the chief with all his images piled at the feet of the large ju-ju in front of his house. First we knelt in prayer and then I asked the chief why he wished to destroy his idols. He said that he had finished with all Satan's ways and that these things could not save him and that he had put his trust in God's Son. Before the assembled members of his household, he took a big stick and broke the objects he had worshipped all his life. The people looked on in awe. We visited room after room where clay gods that had never moved were broken to pieces and scattered to the winds.

People with charms on their persons tore them off and threw them away. We visited another house where a similar performance was carried out. I thought we were through, when a third man said, "Are you ready?"

I asked, "For what?"

He said he wished me to come to his house where, after prayer, a huge idol in clay and many small ones were demolished. So I returned, praising God for a movement that seems of the Holy Spirit in answer to much prayer."

11

JUREMIKO

Juremiko was just a little boy, about eight or nine years of age, when his father threw him out of the house. His father was a rough man and when Juremiko did something that displeased him, he chased him away in a rage. He ran into the forest, not sure where to go or how to get help. Although, like every young Lobi boy, he knew the forest well, he wandered so far that eventually he realised that he was lost.

He didn't know, of course, but God knew exactly where he was and sent an uncle of his out into the forest paths. As God intended, they met and Juremiko's uncle asked where he was going.

"My father has thrown me out of the house," the little boy replied, rather forlornly.

His uncle, for one reason or another, decided not to bring him back to his father's house but instead took him to his own home, in the village of Bouroum-Bouroum.

A day or two later, Stanley woke up and began to make his preparations for the day when he became aware of a most dreadful smell. He opened the door to trace its cause and there, sitting at the door was a little boy. He thought at first that someone had left him there for Stanley and Alice to look after but, when he brought him inside and began to treat the ulcer that had caused the bad smell, he discovered that this was not the case. The boy's name was Juremiko.

Stanley listened to his story as he dressed the heel, which had been wounded on his wanderings in the forest. He told Stanley that he was staying with his uncle and it was arranged that he would call at the Benington house each morning to have the dressing changed.

When he saw the boys who came to the house to learn to read, he asked if he could join them. He proved to be an able student who learnt to read very quickly and was soon able to read all the Bible verses that Stanley had written down.

Some of the other boys began to separate themselves from the pagan practices as they came to understand more about God. The headmen of the village were understandably angry at this situation and the chief of the district eventually issued an ultimatum.

"Any boy who goes back to Daouda's house to learn to read will be killed!"

The boys knew that this was no idle threat so they stopped coming. Stanley was disappointed, but simply waited to see what God would do.

One night there was a tap at the back door. When Stanley opened it, he saw Juremiko.

"Daouda, will you teach me to read?" he asked.

Stanley said to him,

"You know what the chief said."

"I know," Juremiko replied, "but I want to go on with my reading."

So, whenever the young boy had the chance, he would slip along to Stanley's house at night, read everything that Stanley had written down and help him to translate the Scriptures. God once again kept His promise about His Word because it wasn't long before Juremiko came to Stanley one day and said,

"Daouda, I want to take the Son of God into my heart."

He accepted Jesus Christ as his Saviour and then, very bravely, witnessed to his decision by refusing to take part in his family's pagan rituals. They persecuted him, they laughed at him, but he refused to go back to the old ways and Stanley had the joy of watching him grow in the faith, Just as he had seen in Nigeria, God Himself began to teach the little boy what it meant to be a Christian. Stanley was careful not to interfere with this process.

One day he arrived at Stanley's house all dressed up – he had on his bow and his quiver of arrows and a belt around his waist.

"Where are you going?" asked Stanley.

"Can't you hear the drums? They are having a big dance and beer drinking in a village about eight miles away."

"So are you going?" Stanley enquired.

"Yes, oh yes," was Juremiko's enthusiastic response.

"Well," said Stanley gently, "let's pray about it."

So he asked the Lord to go with Juremiko, to care for him, to keep him and to use his life as a witness for the Saviour. Juremiko prayed too and then set off quite happily.

About twenty minutes later, he returned.

"Hello," said Stanley, "you're home quickly."

"Oh, I didn't go."

"You didn't go?"

"No," said Juremiko, "when I got halfway there, God spoke to me and told me that was not a place for one of His children to go. So I came back again."

The way God had dealt with him confirmed for Stanley that Juremiko really was a child of God because He had begun to lead him by His Spirit. Stanley consistently used this method of standing back and allowing God to teach His children. He once explained his reasons in a letter home,

"They have, of course, rather crude ideas about things theological, but I do not interfere very much, as it is better for them to have their ideas changed through growth in grace and knowledge of Christ than through my teaching."

On another occasion, Stanley saw him coming running up the path to his house, in great distress, his arm hanging limply at his side.

"Juremiko, what's happened?" he asked.

"Oh, Daouda," he cried, "I was wrestling and the other boy was going to put me down and anger rose up in my heart and I put out all my strength and broke my arm!"

Stanley brought him in and made him lie down on the bed. He put the broken arm in splints and prayed for him.

"I know it was because of my anger," he whimpered. "It's not pleasing to God when a man is angry in that way."

So Juremiko grew strong in his faith and the people of the village watched the life of this little boy, They didn't like what they saw and set about to turn him away from God.

Some time later, he arrived at Stanley's house late at night, once more in great distress. When Stanley questioned him he told him that he was very hungry.

"Why are you hungry? Why don't you go home and get some food?"

"The people have been very wicked with me," he told Stanley. "It is farming time, as you know, and every day at midday, the women bring the food to the men in the fields. When they put mine down in front of me, just as I begin to eat, they say,

'Ha ha! Look at this boy who says he believes in God – he is going to eat food that has been sacrificed to idols.'

Of course, I cannot eat it. For three days they have done that and I am very hungry."

Stanley's instinctive reaction was to go and get some bread from his meat safe at the other end of the verandah, but as he walked along the verandah, the Lord said to him,

"Don't do that, go and pray with him."

He was so taken aback by this instruction that he argued with the Lord.

"I can't just pray with him when I have food in the house I can give him."

But the Lord's voice was insistent,

"You just go and pray with him."

Stanley was always concerned to be obedient, so even though he felt very mean, he went back to the boy and said,

"You say you're hungry and the people won't give you proper food. Let's tell the Lord about it."

So, still feeling very bad about it, Stanley knelt on the verandah to pray.

"Juremiko, you pray," he suggested. "Do you believe that Jesus Christ has risen from the dead and has all power in heaven and on earth?"

"Yes," affirmed Juremiko.

"Well, tell Him all your trouble."

Stanley listened as the boy told the Lord his story, then he felt the hairs rise on the back of his neck as he heard him say,

"Lord, cause my people to have good food ready for me when I get down to the house tonight."

The boy's house was only about 500 yards from Stanley's, and Stanley knew that it normally took hours to prepare food in a Lobi household.

"The Lord can't do it," he thought but he didn't let his doubts show. He simply prayed too and let Juremiko go on home. Once he had gone, Stanley began to pace up and down the verandah, discussing the matter with the Lord.

"Now Lord, how can this thing be? It is terrible. He is Your child and now he has gone down to his house and they won't have his food ready."

"Did I not send you out here," the Lord replied, "to teach these people about me and do you not teach them that before they call I will answer and while they are yet speaking, I will hear?"

"Yes, Lord, I know - but, alright Lord, we'll leave it and see what happens."

The next morning, long before daylight, there was a knock at the door and there stood Juremiko, his face wreathed in smiles.

"Daouda, it's alright," he said.

"So what happened?" Stanley asked.

"When I got home, they had food ready for me, and …." he laughed triumphantly, "it was food that hadn't been sacrificed to idols!"

So Juremiko learnt that he could depend on the Lord but his uncle's family kept on trying to trip him up. On a later occasion, Stanley had managed to kill three guinea fowl. His father had given him a gun and, as far as possible, he tried to shoot his own meat. He didn't trust the meat on the market stalls, as he reckoned the Lobis never killed an animal if it was a good animal, only if it was sick!

When he returned to his house, he gave one of the birds to Juremiko, who brought it home with him. He went into a quiet corner of the compound and began to pluck the fowl. All at once, the women of the house made a run at him with sticks. He jumped over the fence to escape the blows as they shouted after him,

"Don't dare eat that guinea fowl. You know quite well that guinea fowl is taboo to your family and you have no right to eat it. If you eat it, you'll die!"

Juremiko made his way down to the swamp, where he plucked the fowl, lit a fire and ate the forbidden meat.

Next morning, he went up to Stanley's house quite early and he asked Stanley to pray with him as he had a bad headache.

"What have you done to get a headache?" asked Stanley.

"Well, you know that guinea fowl you gave me yesterday?" he said and he told Stanley the story.

"To eat something that is taboo to the family is a very bad thing and this headache has come because of that."

"Juremiko," Stanley asked, "didn't the Son of God die for you?"

"Yes."

"And He has forgiven all your sins?"

"Yes,"

"And didn't He rise again from the dead?"

"Yes."

"Well then, He has the power over life and death and all evil?"

"Alright then, let's pray about it".

The two knelt together, as they had done so often before, and almost before they had finished praying, Juremiko announced,

"Daouda, my headache has gone!"

So, little by little, Juremiko learnt that his faith really worked, that his God could be trusted, even though he couldn't see Him. It was a hard lesson for someone who had been taught to trust in idols and ju-jus that could be seen – stones, bottles, little pieces of animal skin and gods made of clay. Even though he couldn't see Him, Juremiko proved time and time again that He was there – to guide, to protect, to comfort, to display His power and His glory.

Stanley could hardly have realised, while he was discipling this little boy who had not yet even reached his teens, that he would grow up to be God's gift to the church in Lobiland. Before that time came, however, he had many more lessons to learn – some of them would be harder to learn than others.

12

DJORO

Stanley watched with growing interest as the old man slowly made his way to the front of the house. He was bent over, walking awkwardly with his head stuck out at an angle. He had a cow skin thrown over his shoulder, but wore no other clothing. As he came closer, Stanley could see that he had only one good eye – the other bulged out from the socket. He was carrying his bow and arrow and stool. The man knocked the step and Stanley went out to greet him.

The customary greetings over, the man, who was a witchdoctor in a nearby village, came straight to the point of his visit.

"Daouda," he said, "I hear you have got a word from God."

"Yes, indeed I have, Kenaphue, " Stanley assured him, "that's just exactly what I've got – a word from God."

"Will you tell it to me?" he asked.

"I will – sit down."

Kenaphue took his stool off his shoulder and sat down to listen. Stanley started as near the beginning as he could and told him who God was, how the world had been created and how sin entered God's beautiful world. He told him the story of Jesus and God's plan of salvation. The old man asked no questions, just listened quietly.

When Stanley finished, he said,

"Daouda, I believe this word, I believe it is God's word. Will you come over and destroy my idols for me."

"Not on your life," replied Stanley, "I won't touch your idols." Kenaphue was surprised by this answer – surely the missionary would be glad to destroy his idols.

"Why not?" he enquired.

"Because they are the things *you* believe in."

The old man gave this idea some consideration, then he asked,

"Will you come over and watch me doing it?"

Stanley smiled, "Yes, certainly, I will come over in the morning. I'll be there when the sun rises."

Next morning, Stanley rode his bicycle the five miles to the witchdoctor's village and found that he had an amazing collection ready to be destroyed. He had a goatskin bag, which was filled with all kinds of charms, little brass lizards and all kinds of beautifully made objects. Stanley would have dearly loved to keep some of them as curios but he was well aware of the strong warnings in the Bible against such a practice:

"You shall not bring the abomination of the heathen into your house".

So Kenaphue set about the destruction of his idols. What he couldn't burn in the fire, he buried or beat to dust with a large stick. Then he slowly walked over to the two big idols in front of the house. These were the idols of life and death, very powerful ju-ju indeed. He raised his axe to strike them, then began to tremble.

"Daouda," he whispered, "is there a power that is equal to the power of the spirits in this idol?"

"Kenaphue," said Stanley, "I've told you that the Son of God died for you and that He rose from the dead and that all power has been given to Him. If you want to destroy your idols, destroy them in the Name of the Son of God. Let's kneel down together and pray."

They knelt together in the sand, Stanley prayed and Kenaphue prayed. Then the witchdoctor lifted his axe once more, the trembling gone. He struck an almighty blow to the head of one of the idols and stood watching to see what would happen. When he realised that nothing was going to happen to him, he went ahead and destroyed everything. He brought out his special pot of spirit water from the idol room where he had done his divining. When the spirit water was rubbed on his face, it enabled him to see the spirits. As Stanley watched in astonishment, Kenaphue carried out of that little dark room, thirty-five different idols of every shape and form – monkeys, birds, snakes, fish and many others. One by one, they were beaten into powder and the job was done.

With glad hearts, the two men then dedicated the room to the worship of the Lord and from then on, Christian services were held instead of pagan sacrifices.

In the days that followed, a warm friendship sprang up between the old witchdoctor and the white missionary. Stanley visited his home often and soon his wife also turned from idols to trust in the Son of God and together they witnessed to His power in the little village where they lived. But the evil one who had held them in bondage for so long wasn't pleased. He would bide his time and, one day, he would do his best to capture them again.

As he became more and more proficient in the Lobi language, Stanley was able to understand better how they thought on a spiritual level. He learnt that they believed in a Supreme Being. The name they used for him was Thangba and they thought of him as the creator and understood him to be "there", but had no appreciation of a God who was loving, or kind, or personal. They would not think of turning to him for help when in need or in trouble but in their own way they tried to honour him by doing everything "in his name". There are still many people in the Lobi people group who follow these same traditional beliefs today.

The Lobis also called rain "Thangba" and saw their god expressing himself in the rain that was so necessary for life. When Stanley learnt of this association of their god with rain, he understood the full significance of the question asked to him during the first drought,

"Are you stopping the rain (or Thangba)?"
In one sense they were really asking,

"Have you power over the supreme being in whom we believe?"
Knowing this helped him to understand why there had to be faith in

Jesus before there could be rain and even why God had chosen that particular time to break through in power among the Lobis.

They also believed in a powerful evil spirit, Djoro, and Stanley felt that this was probably as close as possible to our understanding of Satan. This was the spirit from whom all evil came, the lord of all the spirits of the dead. All Lobis were initiated into the people group in the name of Djoro. The ceremonies took place (and still take place today) every seven years and everyone had to go, particularly the children who had never attended. After congregating in the sacred wood near Bouroum-Bouroum, they headed into the bush in the northern part of their area, where they stayed for six to eight weeks. It was a dreadful ordeal and many died as a result of hunger, sickness or exposure. The ceremonies were all designed to give the children a fear of the spirit of Djoro that would haunt them for the rest of their lives.

On their return, the newly initiated boys wore wonderful headdresses made from feathers, not unlike those worn by Native American chiefs, while the girls wore costumes made from long strings of cowrie shells. They would congregate in the market place and celebrate the end of the ceremony. Some, however, never returned, beaten to death or poisoned, and if death occurred during this period, no mourning or funeral ceremonies were allowed – the Djoro had done what was right and mourning would only bring sickness on the family.

The Lobis also believed that the spirits of the dead wandered about for a year and then inhabited the idols, to which the Lobis made sacrifices so that their ancestors would not bring trouble on them. They believed that the spirits could come back as "little people" or "konteebis", who lived in groves and could do all sorts of mischief.

Stanley learnt that there was one of these spirit groves near his house, when he talked one day with a man who was visiting Bouroum-Bouroum. This man was a Christian but had been steeped in paganism before his conversion. His wife had a son, who became ill, so the two of them went to see if Stanley could give them some medicine to help him. Stanley and others prayed many times for the child, but with no success.

Then one day, as he passed the door of the mission house, Stanley noticed something very strange about the basket in which they were carrying the baby – there was an arrow sticking out of it!

"What is the arrow for?" asked Stanley.

"Don't you know there are konteebis living in the grove near here? If I didn't have that arrow in the basket, they might easily have dropped down on the basket and done the baby some harm."

"Well" said Stanley, looking meaningfully at him, "isn't it a good thing you had that because God couldn't have looked after the baby. He would have needed that arrow sticking out there."

The man realised at once what Stanley was saying and removed the arrow. The child soon got better and Stanley kept the arrow as a reminder of what had happened and as an illustration of how completely the people were bound up in the power of the Djoro.

B

TAUGHT BY THE SPIRIT

Benko lived at Jurenkera, a village about fifteen miles away from Bouroum-Bouroum. He arrived at Stanley's house one day, anxious to hear the Word of God. When he heard the good news about Jesus, he asked if Stanley would go to his village to witness the destruction of his idols and so, very early the next morning, Stanley set out on his bicycle. The villagers showed him Benko's house, where Benko and his wife greeted him.

Stanley found them to be an exceptionally pleasant couple, more refined than many other Lobis. The people of the village watched as they painstakingly searched for all their idols and destroyed them. They brought idols down from the roof, and from all the inner rooms of the house. Benko's wife found the little idol she had hidden near her cooking place, so that the evil spirits wouldn't spoil the food. When they had finished, Benko's brother approached Stanley and said that he too wanted to destroy his idols. So the whole process began again and it was midday before they finally destroyed the last idol.

Stanley was hungry and tired by this time and when the young couple invited him to eat with them, he was happy to accept. He nursed the baby while the preparations were made for the meal. He noticed Benko's wife reaching up into the rafters and bringing down a big block of what looked like stone. She chopped bits off it and added them to the soup. Stanley wondered just what he would be eating! He was more familiar with the Lobi porridge she made to go with the soup and was soon enjoying his meal, sticking his fingers into the ball of porridge, pulling a piece off, ramming his thumb into the middle of it and dipping it into the soup. Then Benko offered him a piece of the meat – the stone like substance stored in the rafters. It was like chewing a piece of bark and Stanley was afraid he would break his teeth on it but he did manage to eat some of it. When he asked what meat it was he was told that it was wild pig – a new culinary experience for Stanley.

When the people of the village realised that Benko and his wife had come to no harm through turning from their idols, they almost all decided to become Christians too. Stanley tried to visit them as often as possible, teaching them and sharing his translation of Bible verses as he went along. Sometimes he found it difficult to know just how much he should teach them about doctrine and how much he should leave them to be taught by the Holy Spirit Himself. He experienced this problem when he translated the verse from James chapter 5, which says:

"Is there any sick among you, let him call for the elders of the Church and they will pray over him and anoint him and the prayer of faith shall save the sick."

"Well," he thought, "what am I going to do with that? Maybe I'd better tell them that the time for these things has passed, that it was all right in the Apostolic Church but it doesn't work now. But if I say that, then that must apply to everything else that was said in the Apostolic Church – I can't select the bits I don't want to believe and say the rest is true but this isn't. I think I'll not tell them anything – I'll just translate it and read it to them because it is by faith and if they believe it, it ought to work."

So Stanley did as he had planned and he noticed that they all pricked up their ears when they heard those words. They took God at His word and they prayed for the sick and they saw people healed. Several people in the last stages of pneumonia recovered, women who had difficulties in childbirth were prayed for and delivered their babies safely and Stanley and Alice saw God answer their prayers for their own children on many occasions.

One of the new converts, a lovely humble man, was bitten by a viper one night. He had gone to visit someone and on the way back was bitten by a black mamba. The Lobi word for it was "donphana" which meant "I must burst out in blisters". A bite from this particular viper was usually fatal – death occurred within three days. According to Lobi custom, every man's body was owned by someone else in the people group and the owner of this man's body was a pagan man. He immediately brought the witchdoctors to the man's house, intending to make sacrifices and put medicine on him, in an attempt to cure him.

"No, you're not," protested the Christian man, "I have my trust in the Lord Jesus Christ and I'm not going to have any sacrifices made."

Instead, the Christians prayed for him to get better and within a few days, he was completely well again.

They discovered, of course, that healing didn't always come as a result of prayer and Stanley sometimes worried that this would affect their faith. One man, called Jawmeyte, put his trust in Christ and began to attend the meetings regularly. When he missed a couple of Sundays, Stanley went out to his village to find out what was wrong. He didn't find Jawmeyte, but was told that his baby was sick. A few days later, he strode in to Stanley's house. He was a big, powerful man and his whole demeanour spoke of grim determination, as if to say,

"Let nobody stand in my way, I'm going right through."

"Well," said Stanley, "how are you?"

"I am not well."

"What's wrong?"

"It is my baby," Jawmeyte replied sadly. "My baby is sick and it is going to die."

"Have you prayed?" asked Stanley.

"Yes, I have prayed, but God won't hear."

"All right," said Stanley, "let's tell Him about it."

They knelt together and prayed and told the Lord all about it and asked Him to do what He saw best. Jawmeyte went home and Stanley paced up and down the verandah, pleading with God on the baby's behalf.

"Now Lord, " he reasoned, " here's Your chance. There is a man who needs something to prove to him that You are the Living Saviour. Now if that baby dies, Lord, that's a man who won't be able to stand up. You know quite well he will go back to his idol worship unless you save his baby because that baby is everything to him. His wife has never had a baby before and they have been married a long time. This baby is extremely important to him and it will be a grand proof of Your love to him and Your willingness to answer his prayers."

Then he sensed the Lord saying to him,

"Just wait a minute now, will you not leave me to carry out my purposes?"

"But Lord, " Stanley argued, "If the baby isn't better, how will Your purposes be carried out?"

"Leave that to me," the Lord replied, "Just you pray that My will may be done in this matter and the purpose for which I have allowed the baby to be sick may be worked out through its sickness."

Stanley still wasn't very happy about it all but he knew that the Lord would do the right thing anyway.

As Jawmeyte had feared, the baby died but Stanley was amazed to see that instead of going back to his pagan ways, Jawmeyte's faith seemed to be made stronger by the trial he had faced and he drew closer to the Lord than ever before.

Often when Stanley was teaching, someone would interrupt with a question. Although it was usually little to do with what he was trying to teach, he would stop and answer the question because he found that to be the best way for the people to learn. On one occasion, they were sitting around learning how to sing some choruses, when Benko interrupted with a question.

"Daouda," he asked, "is it right if a man who is a Christian and his brother who is a Christian, never speak to each other?"

Stanley turned the question back on himself,

"What do you think?"

"I don't think it is right," Benko said.

Stanley agreed, "How can it be right if the same Saviour who saves you saves the other man and you don't talk to each other?"

"That's true...... You see Tiltite over there?"

Stanley nodded.

"Well, we haven't spoken for twenty years, we haven't drunk together for twenty years."

Stanley knew enough of the Lobi customs by this time to recognise the significance of what Tiltite was saying. The Lobi phrase for the need for reconciliation was "we don't hold the same calabash". If two people wished to be reconciled, they would hold the same calabash and drink from it, passing it from one to the other.

"Well," Stanley suggested, "why don't you and Tiltite make things right between you both now?"

The two men immediately got up and shook hands and from that moment on the feud was over. Some time later, Stanley heard Benko praying and his heart rejoiced when he realised how God was working in his life.

"You know, Lord," he said, "when we threw away our idols, we thought that was all there was to it but ever since that day, I have seen the filth coming out of my life and my heart."

14

A NEW HELPER

"Having been brought face to face with the awful need, he cries from a burdened heart for workers. These must be men willing to rough it and do pioneering, and they must have a thorough knowledge of the French language...............

We appeal to our friends to make this need known, to tell others about it and to join us in supplication for men with the necessary qualifications.

These French Colonies are a reproach to the Church of Christ. Whilst parts of Southern Nigeria are overcrowded by Missions, the people in the French Colonies have been largely neglected and, as Mr Benington says, more than half have now gone over to the Muslim religion through the sinful negligence of the Churches at home."

This powerful appeal for workers appeared in the Qua Iboe Mission Quarterly soon after Stanley began his work in Lobi land. Stanley felt that they needed at least ten men to make any sort of impact on the area and invited his prayer partners to pray to that end.

A young Scottish man answered the call. His name was Hugh Hamilton and he set sail for Africa on 18th March 1933. Stanley made the long journey to the French port of Grand Bassam to meet him and bring him with great rejoicing to their home at Bouroum-Bouroum.

Alice's quiet but very warm welcome and Stanley's sense of fun helped him to settle in to the strange new life among the Lobis. They introduced him to the mysteries of a mosquito net, they encouraged him to taste the new foods on offer, they sympathised with him when he succumbed, as do most new missionaries to West Africa, to the aches and pains and fever of his first malaria attack. He made friends with Russell and baby June and with the many Lobi children who often came to play with them.

Hugh heard from Stanley and Alice how God had been blessing their ministry,

"There are now eight families in Banlo who have professed faith since the chief and the witchdoctor turned away from their idols," Stanley told him with great delight, "and just before I set off to collect you, we had a visit from a young man who lives at Jurenkera, a village about ten miles from here. He too had heard the Gospel and wanted to destroy his idols. He's a fine looking man – very intelligent – and he grasped the meaning of salvation in no time at all. Within a few days he had got rid of all his ju-jus. Mind you, it hasn't been easy for him. He has had to suffer a lot. I'll bring you to Jurenkera to meet him some day."

Soon Hugh was witnessing at first hand what before had only been stories in the Quarterly Magazine. He and Stanley visited Jurenkera and were greatly encouraged to hear that the first convert had brought his older brother and a neighbour to the Lord. By the end of May that year, there wasn't an idol left in the village!

He met two men who travelled twenty–five miles to invite Stanley to witness the destruction of their household idols. He watched with growing admiration as he saw the strength of their faith being tested through persecution and illness

Hugh also got down to the serious business of learning the Lobi language. He accompanied Stanley on his trips into the bush, meeting chiefs and practising the phrases he had learnt, observing customs and getting used to the culture. Certain aspects of the culture were harder to accept than others. In one of his earliest letters home, he wrote,

"I have been here long enough to see a change in the lives of those who have professed to follow Christ. They have been able to overcome trials and persecutions. When anything is stolen, or anyone threatened, they unite in prayer. We do not have the killing of twins, but if two children die in succession, the third is given a little time, then taken to an ant hill. If the child cries when the ants begin to bite, it is brought home; but if it does not cry, it is left there, as the people say it has an evil spirit which makes it desire to die."

In October and also in December, Mr. Roseberry, the Chairman of the Christian Alliance Mission, paid a visit to Bouroum-Bouroum. They were delighted to welcome him and show him around their village. He was especially pleased to be introduced to Tigite and was greatly impressed by "his glowing witness", and quickly recognised that "his fervour, his prayer, and his shining face are an inspiration to all."

During his visits, Mr. Roseberry spoke at various meetings and some of the Sunday School class became Christians as a result. By this time about thirty families had been impacted by the Gospel and Mr Roseberry was thrilled to be able to meet many of them.

Between the two visits, Stanley and Alice and the two children paid a visit to Ouagadougou, where they stayed for a while at the Alliance mission station. It was a much needed and much appreciated break. Even Stanley found the climate at Bouroum-Bouroum difficult to cope with but it was particularly difficult for Alice and the children. They struggled with the heat and stomach upsets and fevers that left them tired and weak.

They returned from their holiday refreshed and eager to continue the Lord's work in their "prepared place". The little group of Christians welcomed them back with great joy and Stanley was encouraged to see that some of them had made progress in prayer during his absence, though he was disappointed that one of the converts from Mr Roseberry's ministry had still not given up his idols. Fear of the idol's power was still strong among the people.

One thing that really rejoiced his heart was that the Christians at Jurenkera had decided to form a Church. In Stanley's typically understated way, he described this historic moment as "quite an event", adding in his report to the mission magazine,

"It has brought joy to our hearts that amongst these fierce and naked people, there are those who are ready to go the whole way for Christ."

When he spoke to the believers at Bouroum-Bouroum, they too expressed a desire to form a church, so Stanley talked to them about baptism and its meaning. After the service, the oldest convert, Chief Bifielte, stood up to speak.

"Daouda," he said, "the word you have spoken rejoices my heart. I would be glad to be counted amongst those who will join the Church."

In the days that followed, all the young men who attended Stanley's reading class twice a week put their names down for a baptism class. Of course not every convert was prepared to take this step of commitment. Many of them had more than one wife and this created a problem. Membership of a church would necessitate Christian marriage but some of the converts were not prepared to deal with the issues involved in choosing one wife and making provision for the others. Stanley recognised the magnitude of some of these decisions and wisely left God's Spirit to lead His people in the right direction. His letters home requested "earnest, persisting prayer on behalf of these babes in Christ".

15

PATIENCE REWARDED

There was much to encourage Stanley and Alice – the first Lobi Church had been formed, the first missionary recruit had arrived and the first chapters of the Bible had been translated. It was an exciting, fulfilling time to be in Lobi land. The powers of darkness however, weren't pleased to have their hold on the people broken and their opposition manifested itself in various ways. The new converts faced great persecution – many were beaten or even threatened with death.

For Stanley and Alice the opposition took a different form. Alice and the two children continued to be unwell and it became increasingly apparent that they were not going to get better in the harsh climate of Upper Volta. Eventually, their doctor suggested that the only solution was would to go home to Northern Ireland. They agonised about the situation for some months, hoping and praying that they would see an improvement but eventually some difficult decisions had to be made.

They didn't want to live thousands of miles apart but could see no other way ahead. Both Alice and Stanley were totally convinced of their call to Africa and obedience to that call ranked high on their list of priorities. So, even though it was a painful decision to make, they decided that Alice should return home to Ireland with Russell and June. Stanley travelled with them to the coast and then made the long journey back to Bouroum-Bouroum to a house that was strangely quiet without the sounds of his little ones at play. Alice and the children arrived home at the end of June.

They kept in touch, of course, by letter and Stanley soon had some interesting news for Alice. The houseboy who had caused them so much heartache, Koulemba, stayed on with Stanley after Alice went home. One day, when Stanley was writing a letter to Alice, he came in to the room.

"Excuse me, Daouda, are you writing to Madame?" he asked.

Stanley looked up at the very dignified young man in front of him – he was no longer a little boy. Koulemba had grown up and matured in recent days.

"Yes, I am," Stanley replied.

"Well, Daouda," Koulemba went on quietly, "I want you to ask her to forgive me for the way I treated her."

"What do you mean?"

"Let me tell you what it was. I used to go into the services, as you know."

Stanley nodded in agreement.

"I read what I could manage to read in French from the Word of God and I was sure that this was the right way but I did not want to give up my Muslim faith. So I prayed to God and said 'if this is not the right way, then make Madame send me away. If it is the right way, let her keep me on.'"

"So, what happened?" asked Stanley. He had a good idea what had happened, but he wanted to hear it from Koulemba himself.

"'Well, I think you know," the young man went on. "I did everything in my power to annoy Madame. I broke things, I burnt things when I was cooking and did everything I could to get her to send me away because I didn't want to believe that Jesus' way was the right way. But she didn't send me away, as you know."

Stanley remembered Alice's patient acceptance of all the broken dishes and burnt food and thanked God for her tolerance and love. Koulemba's story wasn't finished, however.

"Even that wasn't enough to convince me and I was thinking about it all one day when I went down to the marsh to wash my clothes. You know the big mantle that I wear on Sunday?"

Stanley nodded – it was a beautiful, hand-embroidered garment.

"Well," Koulemba continued, "I took it with me and set it down beside the water. It was towards the end of the rainy season and the waters were flowing out of the marsh. I put it down beside me and somehow the water got hold of it and swept it away. Immediately I prayed and said, 'Oh God, if the Jesus way is the true way, let me find my mantle again.' Just as I was praying, I felt the mantle winding itself around my legs and I knew this really was the living way. So I want you to apologise to Madame for me."

Stanley was happy to send Koulemba's apologies home to Alice – he was only sorry that she was not there to see the change in him for herself. He accepted Jesus as his Saviour and was a fearless witness for Him. Soon after his conversion, he travelled the fifteen miles to Gaoua, where he found all his Muslim friends and told them about Jesus and his newfound faith.

"Well," they said, "in that case, you are going to hell. Don't ever come near us again."

From that time on, none of his friends would shake hands with him or speak to him. He was forced to make new friends among the Lobi people, which proved difficult because he didn't know the language well. He persevered, however, and often Stanley would see him talking about Jesus to the people in Bouroum-Bouroum. And each time he did, Stanley would remember again that Alice's patience and longsuffering had been links in the chain that led him to Jesus.

Alice also had some exciting news for Stanley in one of her letters – they were to be parents again!

16

FAITH TESTED

The work at the village of Jurenkera continued to prosper. One of the last men to throw away his idols was Tiltite, the brother of Benko. Stanley described him as a "dark-faced man who had a dour, unattractive character." At the time of his conversion, before Alice had gone home, they hadn't been too sure if he had simply followed the lead of his brother, when he had put away his idols – somehow it hadn't seemed to be a true conversion.

Soon afterwards he fell ill and when he didn't seem to be recovering, he talked about going back to idol worship. He complained that God wasn't treating him properly. Stanley and Alice prayed earnestly for him, and with him, and he recovered from his illness. He became ill the following year, this time with a different illness, and once again he got discouraged and thought about bringing back his idols. This time the Lord healed him in a wonderful way and Stanley and Alice noticed an improvement in him after that.

Then, one Sunday, he arrived at the Church service, his face dark with anger.

"Thieves broke in to my farm last night!" he shouted. "I'll kill them if I find them."

According to the old Lobi customs, he would have been within his rights to do so and Stanley's heart sank to hear this further indication that Tiltite still hankered after the old ways. His anger was apparent in his prayer too.

"God, don't let that thief escape from me!"

Stanley pointed out after the service that his attitude was all wrong and reminded him that Christ had freely forgiven his sins but Tiltite was set on revenge.

A couple of weeks later, God convicted him about his anger and he confessed his sin in the service, asking the Christians to pray for him. A remarkable transformation took place – Tiltite's health improved almost immediately and over the months that followed, his character changed under the influence of the Spirit of God and the old threatening look left his face.

The next year, Tiltite was blessed with another good crop of yams. Once again a thief broke in and stole many yams from his farm. Stanley told the story of what happened in a report sent to the Mission Quarterly.

"It is again yam season and Tiltite has once more a good crop. One morning very early, he sees in his farm a thief who carries away a load of these precious vegetables. Knowing the man, he goes off to the chief of his village and asks for the return of the stolen goods.

The chief, the man and all in the village deny any knowledge of the theft. They are heathen and not friendly with the Christians of Jurenkera. However, they are willing to put the matter to the test.

Tiltite knows the custom. He has only to go and get a young chicken and bring it to the chief's yard. The chief will call the accused man to bring his chicken and the matter will be put to the trial of the evil spirit. Tiltite refuses. Well, if so, there is an end to the matter.

But no. Let the heathen hold his chicken and Tiltite will pray to God in the Name of His Son to show the truth of the matter. They agree, believing that only Satan has the power to reveal, by the manner in which a chicken dies, who is the culprit.

The witch doctor is called. The stage is set. They go through their incantations. Before the chicken is sacrificed, and in the presence of all the heathen, and alone, Tiltite kneels down and asks God in the Name of His Son, to show that He has the power to prove that this man is the thief.

The knife is whipped out, the blood flows, the chicken is thrown down at the altar and all watch breathlessly to see whether it will die on its back and so indicate the thief. Imagine the joy of the lone believer and the astonishment of the heathen, when with a quiver, the chicken rolls over and dies with its legs stuck up in the air.

Evidently all is not right. The case must be tried again. Again and again it is tried with the same result. At last they take the matter to the head District Chief. Here the same performance is gone through and the believer in the Son of God kneels once more in opposition to all the forces of darkness and once more he is vindicated.

Tiltite comes home rejoicing to tell the Christians of his village that vengeance belongs to the Lord and he does repay.

This is all the more delightful to us, as we did not know anything about the matter until it was all over. He did not consult us at all but went the way he felt the Lord would have him go. It is a great testimony, as just a week earlier, he was reproving another Christian for anger against a man who had wronged him. He little thought how soon the Lord would test him in a similar way.

And so they grow through adversity and opposition and trial. How wonderful is the quiet operation of the Holy Spirit. How well we may trust Him to complete the work that He has begun in the hearts of these children of the Light, who once were sunken in such depths of darkness."

About the same time as his article was published in the magazine, Stanley began to feel unwell. Hugh helped to nurse him as best he could but the fever had taken its toll on him and it was decided that Stanley should return home a little earlier than planned so that he could recuperate. He arrived home on 27th December 1934 and booked in for a course of treatment at the Hospital for Tropical

Diseases in London. How wonderful it was to be reunited with Alice and the children again. What stories they had to share. His earlier return also meant that he was at home for the birth of their third child, a son, Maurice, born in a nursing home on the 19th January 1935.

Having recovered sufficiently well to take meetings, he began a period of deputation, anxious to encourage other Christian men and women to take up the challenge of Upper Volta. He was one of the speakers at the Portstewart Convention in June, an event which brought back memories of God's call on his life many years previously. How he prayed that God would do it again, that lives would be touched, that others would give their lives to bring the Gospel to the Lobi people. Those who heard him speak remarked on the passionate and powerful way in which he presented the challenge of missionary service but no one responded by offering to join him.

He was also invited to speak at the annual meeting of the Worldwide Evangelisation Crusade in London. After his great investigative journey through West Africa, Stanley had gone to the W.E.C. headquarters in London and had laid the need in West Africa before the W.E.C. leader, Norman Grubb. So Norman issued the invitation to him to speak about his journey and to appeal for workers. Though he didn't realise it for some time, that meeting would be the means God would use to touch the heart of a young man who would eventually spend forty years of his life serving God among the Lobis.

Meanwhile, back in Upper Volta, Hugh had moved into the Beningtons' house while Stanley was away and continued to visit the little groups of Christians in the surrounding villages. He was friendly with Benko and some of the other Christians and, as a result of their ministry, the work progressed and people continued to turn from their idols to serve the True God.

Hugh became concerned about a pain in his side, until in August the pain had become so bad that he made the trip to Bobo to have it investigated in the hospital there. The diagnosis was appendicitis, so he had an operation to remove his appendix. He made a good recovery and it seemed that everything was back to normal.

In December, he sent an encouraging report to his prayer partners at home, mentioning the profitable services at Gaoua and the refreshing time of fellowship he had had at the recent Christian Missionary Alliance Conference at Kankan. He also reported some rather unnerving experiences he had undergone.

Someone came to tell him about the death of an old blind man in Pan'jala. He had been a Christian as had his seventeen-year-old son, who wanted his father to have a Christian burial. The heathen relatives disagreed and took the body away. They went through the usual pagan ceremonies including the "questioning" of the corpse. This ritual involved the corpse being carried around the people, answering questions put to it by jerking the bearers down to one or other side. When his relatives told him what the corpse had been "saying", he was so frightened that he made an idol and sacrificed to it.

They then went to two other Christian families and began to threaten them too, at which point a man was sent to Bouroum-Bouroum to tell Hugh. The young missionary felt that it was his duty to go to the village and set out immediately. On arriving at the chief's house, he greeted him and then found the young boy, who spoke to Hugh and agreed to meet with him the next day.

Morning came but the boy did not turn up – he had fled from the village. Hugh heard that he had been told that he would be killed if he spoke to the missionary again. Hugh tried to make contact with those who were causing all the trouble but they had disappeared off into the bush. There was little more he could do, so he gathered the Christians together, prayed with them and went back to Bouroum-Bouroum. When he talked to Tigite about the threats, he warned Hugh that the men causing the trouble were a treacherous lot.

Hugh also wrote about his plans to go back to the area at the beginning of the year. He was aware that the people in the villages he passed through had viewed him with great suspicion and fear, so he thought that if he spent a couple of weeks travelling around, meeting the people, he might be able to dispel their fear.

It is fortunate indeed that God casts a veil over the future – neither he nor the Beningtons could have coped with knowing what was just around the corner.

17

FOREST FIRE

When the telegram from the Christian Missionary Alliance arrived in the Belfast office of the Qua Iboe Mission on 27th January 1936, it caused shock and disbelief.

"HAMILTON DEAD. CAUGHT BUSH FIRE."

There were no details given, no explanation for his death. For his family, the tragedy was further compounded because his father had died just a few days before the telegram reached the office. His mother, who had been looking forward to her son's return in May for his first furlough, now found herself mourning the loss of both her husband and her son. The editor of The Quarterly Magazine expressed the sentiments of many when he wrote:

"We are dumb in the presence of this tragedy......... We can only say that he has given his life for Christ's cause in Africa. A grain of wheat has fallen into the ground. It will not abide alone, but by the testimony of our brother, his life among the people – now so strangely ended – and by the manner of his death, God will speak and souls will be garnered for His glory."

Hugh's death was, of course, a source of great sorrow and disappointment to the Beningtons. They had hoped that he would be the first of many who would join in the work of bringing the Word of God to Upper Volta. Stanley had greatly appreciated his company when Alice had gone home and had enjoyed training him and teaching him. Now they would have to begin the process all over again.

Stanley's return to the mission house, in May of that year, was a sad one. The home that he and Alice had built together was neglected and dilapidated. As he approached it, he could see that that part of the roof had fallen in and needed to be repaired. The house was sealed up and he had to pay a visit to the police commander to get permission to reopen it. Once inside, he was dismayed to see that the wind had blown Hugh's papers all over the floor and everything was covered in a layer of dust. He wearily cleared a space in the bedroom and fell asleep.

It wasn't until a few days later that he found out what little details were known about Hugh's death. Some of the Christians from the village where he had been living had come in to see him in some distress.

"Uncle Hu," they said, "there is a lion that is eating our cattle. Will you come and shoot it?"

Hugh gathered up his gun and his ammunition and set off on his motorcycle. When he arrived at the village, some of the older men of the church tried to dissuade him from going after the lion.

"This lion is a very wicked creature," they said. "It would be very dangerous to pursue it. We don't want you to get into any trouble. Just leave it to us."

They were concerned that if anything happened to the white man, they would get into trouble with the Government. Hugh was still keen to help, however, so he and a few of the Christians went down into the swamp. The elephant grass in the swamp was very high, as it was the dry season, so it was impossible to see if the lion was still around.

"I'll get up into a tree and see if I can see any sign of it, " said Hugh.

"Oh don't do that," his friends begged him, "it's too dangerous. What if there's a forest fire? What if the lion comes and lies down under the tree and you're not able to shoot it? What if the elephants come and push the tree over?"

Hugh knew that these were very real dangers but went ahead with his plan, assuring them that if there was a fire, he would be able to see it and would get down. He climbed up and began to look for signs of the lion. As he gazed out over the swamp, he noticed a fire starting up in the distance but shouted down that it was a long way off and that he would be all right. He obviously underestimated the speed of a forest fire, because those who were watching a little distance away saw him fall from the branches, possibly overcome by the smoke. They ran to assist him, but the flames beat them to it and they couldn't get near him. When they eventually beat out the flames and pulled him clear, he was barely conscious and talking in English, which they couldn't understand. They sent for a doctor, who lived about thirty miles away, but he could not help him and Hugh died shortly afterwards.

When Stanley heard this sad tale, he wondered for a moment if the pagan people, who had been so antagonistic to Hugh on his last venture into the bush, might have started the bush fire deliberately. There was an official enquiry into his death, but no proper conclusion was ever reached.

Whether or not the powers of darkness were behind Hugh's tragic death, the Christian Church there was badly affected by it. The converts had seen God's power at work in healing and provision and protection and found it hard to accept that in this case, God had chosen not to intervene. Many of them lost their faith and went back to their heathen ways. Others made wrong decisions and missed having access to Stanley's wise counsel. Benko was one of the latter.

Stanley's first visitor after his return from furlough was Benko's wife. They greeted one another and then Benko's wife said,

"Daouda, I am in trouble."

"What's your trouble?" Stanley enquired.

"Benko has taken a second wife," she said.

"But why shouldn't he?" he enquired provocatively.

"Oh, he knows it is wrong," she assured Stanley, "God spoke to him and told him it's wrong and that he shouldn't do it."

Stanley promised to talk to Benko about the matter and prayed with his wife before she set off for home.

A few days later he met Benko and asked him,

"How is your second wife?"

Benko's face fell when he realised that Stanley knew what he had done.

"Oh Daouda, I'm sorry now that I took a second wife."

"Well, " said Stanley, "there's not much use being sorry about it and not doing anything about it."

Benko's brow furrowed. "But what can I do?" he asked.

He thought for a moment, then he had an idea.

"I know," he announced, "I'll flog her every morning and then she'll run away!"

"Well," said Stanley, "do you think that would please God? Don't forget you brought her into your house yourself. She didn't come in without you asking her and if you start flogging her, you are going to commit another sin against God. You shouldn't ill treat a person you brought into your house and made your wife."

Fortunately, Benko saw the sense in what Stanley was saying and so he decided to pray about the situation instead.

They met up again some time later and Benko was sure he had the solution to the problem this time.

"Daouda," he said, "I have thought what to do about my wife."

"Good – what are you going to do?"

"Well, I'll tell you what," he replied, "I have a white hen that is sitting on eggs and I am going to give that to God so that He will forgive me for this."

"And will you keep your second wife?" Stanley asked.

"Yes," said Benko, but he began to look less sure of himself.

"Listen, Benko, can you hold that white hen so near to the face of God that it will hide your wife from His eyes?"

Benko laughed at the very idea.

"No, that's no good."

"No, that's no good, Benko," Stanley agreed. "There is only one thing to do and that is to ask God to show you how you can put this wife away without wronging Him further than you have done already."

"All right," he said, "I will just pray to God that he will deliver me because I have done wrong."

The next thing Stanley heard was that the woman had simply decided herself to leave Benko, without him mistreating her in any way. God had answered his prayer and had sorted out the situation for him. Once his sin had been dealt with, Benko continued to be a great encouragement to Stanley. He was the only one who showed any real interest in learning to read. He would go to Stanley's house as often as he could and Stanley would teach him as much as possible in one sitting. Then Benko would go away and try to teach someone else what he had learnt. It was slow work but progress was made. At the same time, Stanley was translating the Gospel of John, so that when some of the converts did learn to read, there would be at least some of God's Word in their own language for them to read.

RW
2/9/02

18

A FAITHFUL FOLLOWER

Although many of the original converts had returned to their pagan
ways, Stanley was pleased to find that his old friend, Kenaphue,
was still as strong in his faith as ever. He heard that the old man had
had a difficult time while Stanley had been on furlough, so he went
to his house to visit him. His wife, Hinapier, was sweeping out their
little room.

"Where is Kenaphue?" Stanley asked her.

"He is out on his farm," she replied.

After having a chat with her, Stanley walked on down the narrow
track in the dry, dusty earth to Kenaphue's farm. When Stanley saw
him in the distance, bent low over his hoe, he crept up quietly
behind him and just said his name.

Kenaphue straightened up slowly, turned round and looked at
Stanley with his one good eye.

"Daouda," he said, "they told me you were dead."

"No," Stanley assured him, "I'm not dead yet. How are you?"

The two men moved into the shade of a nearby tree and Kenaphue
told him what had happened. The witchdoctors of the area had come
to see him soon after Stanley left.

"Kenaphue," they said, "we'll tell you the truth – that white man who told you that if you believed his word, you would live forever, is himself dead. We know because we have word from his country to say he is dead and will never come back again. Now we want you to reveal your secrets to us, turn back and be one of us again."

Stanley could understand just how anxious they would have been to welcome this old man back into their circle. He had been the head witchdoctor of the whole area and would have known many dark secrets.

"We will give you anything you want if only you will join us again. Look, we've brought you cows and we've brought you new wives. We know you are tired of the old one. Everything will be all right if you will just talk to us."

What a temptation it must have been for Kenaphue, to once again become a wealthy, powerful figure among his people. He must have wondered if what they said was true – after all, hadn't Hugh Hamilton been killed? Had the little group of converts been deserted - left to carry on alone?

Kenaphue refused to entertain these thoughts and told those who gathered around him,

"I will never talk about my secrets again."

The other witchdoctors increased their efforts, tempting him in every possible way, but Kenaphue would not give in to their offers. Hinapier stood with him and encouraged him to remain true. As he sat talking to Stanley, he thought how glad he was that he had not given in to them and believed their lies. All the other converts in his village had gone back to their pagan ways – only Kenaphue and his wife remained faithful. It had been a lonely, difficult time. How glad he was to see his friend once more, having thought for many months that he was dead.

As soon as he got his house into some sort of order, Stanley began holding services on the verandah, just as before and Kenaphue and Hinapier attended regularly. They also held a little service in their own room, as a witness in their village.

One day Kenaphue surprised Stanley by saying,

"Daouda, my day for dying is very near."

"And how do you know that?" enquired Stanley.

"Well," said the old man, "The other night I was lying asleep, when I woke up and saw spirits of dead people standing around the foot of the mat where I was lying. They were the spirits of those I had killed in past days. I saw them all standing round my bed, wanting to take me down into the country of the dead."

"Kenaphue, " said Stanley, "do you believe that the Son of God died for you?"

"I do."

"And that He has forgiven all your sins?"

"Yes, I do."

"And that He rose from the dead and has gone into heaven and is seated at the right hand of God?"

"Yes, I believe all those things," replied Kenaphue, in the tone of one who had answered the same questions many times before.

"Then listen – He has defeated death, the devil and all the evil spirits. Those are not men you see round your bed, those are evil spirits impersonating the people you had killed. A man who dies is there for keeps, he doesn't come out again until it is God's time."

"Now," Stanley went on, "if those spirits come back again, you call on the name of the Son of God and see what happens."

A month or two went by before they met again and Stanley greeted him with the words,

"Kenaphue, you're not dead yet?"

"Ah, no Daouda, I'm not."

"Did the spirits come back?"

"The spirits came back a night or two after we talked and I called on the name of the Son of God and they ran away and I have never seen them since!"

Kenaphue remained a wonderful tribute to the grace of God right to the end. To Stanley, he was proof that no matter what a man was like, no matter what his past had been, if he put his trust and faith in the Son of God, he was a child of God without any possible argument.

Others were not such good examples and an article written for the mission magazine reflected the ups and downs experienced by Stanley during those first months back in Bouroum–Bouroum.

"I went to Jurenkera and when all were gathered, had a good time praying and singing. It is gratifying to see how these Christians have grown and to hear them praying.

..........After this I passed on to see the chief, Djinkur, who took his idols back some time ago. You would not believe the change which has come over him; there is now a dark, fearsome look on his face. The Christians have dealt with him and so I shall leave it at that, as their word will carry more weight than mine.

.........At one of the services in Bouroum-Bouroum, Dakprou openly confessed having fallen into sin by taking part in heathen rites. He became ill and believed that his sickness was the result of his sin. He put his trust in God, who gave him courage to refuse to share in the sacrifices which were made by his friends on his behalf.

............Lastly, I met Jawtinite, and in the course of conversation, found that he had had the grace to refuse food offered to idols. He had also prevented Kidite from eating the same unknowingly.

...........I hear that the teacher at Djiebougou is converted and his wife also. I have asked permission to have services there and I am also hoping to be allowed to build a church at Jurenkera."

Stanley was greatly helped and encouraged at this time by a young English man, Jack Robertson, who had come to help him. On his way back to Lobi land, Stanley had called in at Vavoua to visit Sam Staniford, the Field Leader of the Worldwide Evangelisation Crusade. Sam and his helpers had begun to build a mission station in that part of Ivory Coast and Stanley was keen to see their work. He had a special interest in Sam, as it had been partly in response to Stanley's discussion with Norman Grubb that the Stanifords had been sent to begin the W.E.C. work in West Africa. They were experienced missionaries who had already spent sixteen years in the Congo.

His visit also had a much sadder purpose as he had learnt that Sam's wife had died as a result of yellow fever, while Stanley had been at home on leave and he was anxious to meet with his friend and sympathise with him in his bereavement.

They chatted for some time, then the discussion changed direction and they began to talk about the work they were hoping to do.

"You have two young men working with you," Stanley pointed out, jokingly, " while I'm going to be all alone in Upper Volta. Could one young man not come with me?"

Sam decided that the matter was worthy of some serious thought and before the evening was over, he asked Jack Robertson if he would pray about it. Jack, it turned out, was the young man who had heard Stanley speak at the W.E.C. conference the previous year. He had been the first to respond to God's call to work with W.E.C. in Ivory Coast and while learning French as part of his preparation, had seen a map of Ivory Coast and had somehow felt strangely drawn to the area of the Lobi people group. So God had already prepared his heart for the suggestion made to him by Sam.

The following morning, Jack's reading included the words, "Go with this man and go in his country where you want to go."

Jack accepted this very clear guidance from the Lord and duly arrived in Bouroum-Bouroum on 13th July in 1936. Like Hugh Hamilton before him, he settled down to language study and was soon able to converse a little with the people of the village.

The two men enjoyed a visit in November from a gentleman called Lewis who was touring many of the mission fields in West Africa and who later described his experiences in a book entitled "Missionary Trails". Lewis heard the story of the beginning of the work among the Lobi people group and Stanley, Jack and Juremiko took him on a tour of the village.

They set out in broad daylight and, as they walked through the field of tall corn, Lewis wondered why he had been told to bring a flashlight! He understood the reason, however, when Juremiko invited them to go inside one of the Lobi homes – the house was a maze of rooms all leading from one into another and the interior rooms of the house had no light at all! His first sight of the room containing the household idols made quite an impact on him:

"As we came to a side room, Mr Benington pointed into the door and said 'You lead the way.' I went ahead, casting the flashlight

beam around to see what I was coming to. On the ceiling I saw hundreds of bats hanging head down from the ceiling poles. As the flashlight beams struck them many dropped from the ceiling and began flying back and forth through the darkness, but as I cast the flashlight beam around I finally saw what Mr Benington had really brought me to observe – a row of hideous idols, perhaps thirty inches high, around the wall of the room. There was no attempt to make them beautiful – simply hideous busts, very crudely made of mud with grotesque feathers and the nearest one covered with fresh chicken blood and feathers, where a blood sacrifice had recently been made.

I had always thought of idol worship as something far off, something we read about in the Bible times, something unreal and mythical, but here I was face to face with it in an idol room, with those bats flying back and forth past our heads in the darkness."

Lewis' comment on the three days he spent in Bouroum-Bouroum offer an interesting insight into Stanley's Godly character:

"How I wish I could convey to my readers the wonderful spiritual blessing and joy which came to me as I spent three days in this place. It is a rare privilege and blessing to spend a few days with such a man of God. His Irish humour was always ready, his conversation quick, sparkling, vivacious; his whole being seemed energetic and full of activity; yet over all was such a wonderful feeling of the immediate presence of God that a veritable spiritual blessing radiated from his personality."

19

HIS PROMISED HUNDREDFOLD

One of Stanley's more frequent visitors at this time was Juremiko, who had been such an encouragement to Stanley before his furlough and who now continued to help him with translation work. He was honest and reliable and Stanley was very pleased to see the progress he was making, both in reading and in his faith.

He came to Stanley one day and announced that he would love to have a bicycle. Stanley's bicycle was the only one in the whole area and Juremiko decided that he needed one too.

"Well", said Stanley, "we'll ask the Lord about it."

"Oh," replied Juremiko, "I have already asked Him and he hasn't said anything. I want to go to Bobo and work there and get money to buy a bicycle."

Stanley was very concerned to hear this, as Bobo was about one hundred and fifty miles away and Stanley knew that Juremiko would face much temptation there. Bobo had a reputation for being a wicked place and it would be hard for a young Christian on his own to maintain his high moral standards.

"If the Lord wants you to go," he told Juremiko, "then go, but don't go if He doesn't want you to go because it won't be a success."

The desire to have a bicycle was too strong and Juremiko set off for Bobo, despite Stanley's warnings about what he might have to face. Some time passed and then Stanley received a rather sad letter from Bobo.

"I have fallen into sin with a girl," he wrote. "I am asking God if He will forgive me. The devil has deceived me into thinking that money was the chief thing in life."

Although Stanley was saddened by his letter, he was also pleased to see that Juremiko recognised what he had done to be sin. Sexual standards among the Lobis were different to Christian standards. Sexual activity usually began during the initiation ceremonies and the children who attended them lived together in the sacred grove on the outskirts of the village for two or three weeks and no restrictions seemed to be placed on their behaviour. The Lobis would not consider such a relationship a sin.

Stanley assured the young man that God would indeed forgive him and invited him to stay at his house for some time. They spent time together, translating the Gospel of John. As each little passage was translated, Juremiko would take it and the translation of "The Way of Salvation" leaflet out to the nearby villages, telling all who would listen to him about Jesus and His love. His mode of transport was Stanley's bicycle – he never did get the bicycle he had gone to Bobo to buy!

Juremiko's allegiance to Jesus was tested soon afterwards. The time for the initiation ceremony came and this caused great controversy in the area. The pagan people were anxious to go ahead with the ceremony but the Christians said they would not join in. The pagans waited and waited, hoping that the Christians would change their minds. The ceremony eventually went ahead in 1937 and Juremiko was the first of the Christians to refuse to attend – a brave action which encouraged others to follow his lead.

In later years, Juremiko married and had four children. He took the Christian name "Job" and became a well–respected Pastor. He continued to be devoted to the Lord and was a faithful witness to Him, leading many people to faith in Jesus. He rose to become the chief Lobi Elder in the town of Gaoua. Stanley often remarked on how wonderful it was to watch him grow into such a fine Christian leader.

"It was such a glorification of the grace of God," he would say. "A wee boy, with a bad, stinking heel, right out in the forests of French West Africa, where there was no one who knew anything about God, except ourselves in Bouroum-Bouroum, fifteen miles away......... The Lord was there, seeking out His sheep. He was working in the heart of Juremiko before he knew anything about it...... He was planning every detail of his walk through the forest, giving him courage in the dark night...... He was working in the heart of that pagan uncle of his, that wicked witchdoctor, bringing him home to the town where we were living."

"Who did that?" he would ask. "Who arranged that?"

"And you know," he would add, "my life was arranged in just the same way. It gives tremendous rest and peace to anybody who can accept the truth of that and walk in it".

At the time, however, his rest and peace were to be severely tested. Alice and Stanley had always assumed that they would be the first of a number of missionaries who would serve the Lord in Upper Volta but since Hugh Hamilton's untimely death, there had been no further applications to the Qua Iboe mission for service among the Lobis.

He was not, of course, working alone, as Jack Robertson had been "loaned" to Stanley for a year, in the hope that by that time, someone else would have arrived from the Qua Iboe Mission. He was extremely grateful for Jack's companionship and help but continued to look for the answer to his prayers for ten men to serve among the Lobis.

He still held to his vision to see three thousand converts among the Lobi people. During his early days among the people group, when he was greatly frustrated by the lack of response among the people, he had been pacing up and down in the moonlight one evening, talking to the Lord about the problem. As he complained to the Lord that He had brought him from a fruitful ministry in Nigeria to a people who wouldn't believe, the Lord reminded him of a verse in Mark's Gospel:

"No one who has left home or brothers or sisters or mother or father or children or fields for Me and the Gospel will fail to receive a hundred times as much in this present age........."

Stanley had taken those words as a promise and there and then he counted up the people he had left behind. He calculated that he had left behind thirty relatives and so he had claimed from God three thousand Lobi converts - his 'hundredfold' – and had believed that they would trust Jesus before he died.

It was hard to see how God would fulfil His promise if the work closed down and the situation puzzled Stanley and distressed him. He could see the tremendous need all around him and found it difficult to understand why others were not responding to that need. He determined to set aside half an hour in the middle of each day for special intercession. He prayed earnestly that the Holy Spirit would convict the people of their need of Jesus and invited his prayer partners at home to join him at the same time each day.

While he waited, he continued to work among the people and to learn more of their customs. His next report outlined some of their strange beliefs about death.

"I took a sick woman to the doctor at Gaoua. She confessed to having eaten her two children! The doctor said she was in the last stages of typhoid and it was too late to save her.

Her remains were brought back in the night and I was awakened by a great cry from the adjacent house. It was the beginning of the mourning for her. When I went over a weird sight met my eyes, with the moonlight falling on the dark, hopeless faces.

About thirty women squatted around the dead form, all wailing in a distressing monotone. Several others walked slowly up and down, with their arms stretched above their heads, as though invoking the heavens to take note of their miserable state, all the time calling the dead girl by name to return.

I went back on the Monday to show my sympathy and sat with a select group to listen to the judging of the dead. I am impressed with the utter mystery of the whole business. The people believe that the corpse has power to control the movements of the bearers. It all seems to show the influence of Satan."

Sitting in the middle of a pagan funeral and witnessing at first hand the hold Satan had on these people, it was hard to hold on to

God's promise that he would reap a "hundredfold". There were many disappointments and frustrations in the work among the Lobis and Stanley's return to the place prepared for him had been tinged with much sadness, but even so, he could end his report on a positive note:

"He has renewed my hope and courage, as I have pleaded His promises. What He has promised He is able to perform, even among the Lobis."

PRW
2/9/02

20

A DIFFICULT DECISION

Stanley became increasingly aware, during that year of waiting, of the possibility that the Qua Iboe Mission would decide to close their operation in Upper Volta. He had met the Home Council during his furlough and there had been a lengthy discussion about the practicality of continuing the work among the Lobis when there was such a great need for workers in Nigeria. At that time it was decided that Stanley should return and that the Mission would publicise the Lobi work in the press and also hold a special meeting in one of the cafes in Belfast, the Merrythought Café.

Stanley had spoken at that meeting and shown slides of his work in Upper Volta, hoping that perhaps some of the students who had been invited would hear God's call. There had been no response, however, to his impassioned pleas for more workers among his beloved Lobis and he often wondered just how God would fill the gap if he had to leave.

As he prayed about the situation, he was reminded that Sam Staniford had a great interest in the work among the Lobis so he wrote to him and suggested that he might like to visit Bouroum-Bouroum once again. Sam agreed and brought a friend with him.

Together they visited the area and discussed the situation at great length with Stanley. Before they left, they had agreed that, should the Qua Iboe Mission pull out, W.E.C. would be prepared to carry on with the work.

Despite knowing of their interest, it was still extremely distressing for Stanley when a letter from the Home Council arrived in the middle of 1937, and he read of their final decision:

"It was unanimously decided that our occupation in Upper Volta should be terminated"

It was suggested that Stanley should finish translating John's Gospel and then plan to return to Nigeria at the end of that year. The work there was growing and they needed more workers to cope with the increasing demands of the newly opened fields in the northern areas of Igala and Bassa. Stanley already knew the language and the culture and would be able to fit back into the team again very quickly.

Stanley really struggled with the decision. He paced up and down outside his house for many hours, going over and over it all in his mind.

"I love these people...... I love this country.......I know the language.... I have so little translation work done ....It has taken so long to learn the Lobi language......... Is that all to be wasted?.......... Why not resign from the Qua Iboe Mission and join the W.E.C. mission and stay here? There is such a need........ If W.E.C. sent a permanent worker, the two of us could get so much done.............. I know God prepared this place for me – does He now want me to leave?"

As he talked it all through with the Lord, he seemed to hear Him say,

"What did I call you to?"

"To the Qua Iboe Mission," he replied.

"Then don't leave the Qua Iboe Mission unless I cause you to leave it," God's voice said clearly. "You obeyed Me in joining the Mission, don't disobey me in leaving it."

That reminder of his original call was really all that Stanley needed. His decision was made – he would go back to Nigeria.

21

A COSTLY BATTLE

The last few months in Bouroum-Bouroum among his beloved Lobi people were busy and sad and difficult. There were so many things he wanted to do before he left. The translation work was a priority, so many hours were spent with Juremiko and another Lobi boy, called Bequoi, reading the Gospel of John in French and discussing the best way to translate it into the Lobi language.

He felt inadequate doing translation work after only six years of language learning, but there was just no one else who could do it, so he tackled the job with his usual enthusiasm and dedication. His task was not made any easier by the frequent attacks of neuralgia that plagued him during those months

"Translation and neuralgia," he declared, "are not good bed-fellows!"

When the final reading of John was finished, Bequoi said to Stanley,

"Daouda, I know that this Book is the truth," and announced his intention of becoming a Christian.

The Gospel was printed by the National Bible Society of Scotland some time after Stanley had left for Nigeria and he wondered if he would ever have the privilege of actually seeing Lobis reading the results of his labour. He also left behind an extensive vocabulary of about three thousand words in the Lobi language – a wonderful help to any missionaries who might follow in his footsteps.

It was with a heavy heart that he said 'goodbye' to the thirty converts who had given their lives to Jesus in the seven years he had been there and to the many young boys he had taught to read. As he visited the villages and called for the last time at the homes of Kenaphue and Tigite and Juremiko, he wondered if he would ever see them again. Perhaps their reunion would have to wait until they were all called home – what a reunion that would be!

He packed up his belongings in his usual meticulous way, handed over the work to Jack Robertson and cast a final glance around the little house that had been home for the past seven years. Despite his personal feelings of regret he was sure that he was doing God's will in returning to Nigeria and he was confident that the amazing God, in whom he believed, was able to provide for the needs of the little groups of Lobi Christians being left behind.

Soon after his departure, Sam Staniford, the field Leader of W.E.C. International, made his way to Bouroum-Bouroum, bringing with him two young men, Frank Miller and Albert Dean. Albert was particularly interested in carrying on Stanley's work among the Lobis. Staniford and Miller stayed for a month before moving on to work in Senegal. Albert Dean began to learn the language, thrilled to be working in a people group he had felt called to some years before. He had arrived in Ivory Coast at the end of January 1938 and his diary entry for the day of his arrival expressed something of his excited anticipation for the task ahead:

"Jan 23: Hallelujah! Our hearts are full of praise to God for bringing us safely to the land of our adoption. As the boat approached the land, I felt an inward joy and sublime peace in leaving all and following Him to this land. The future remains unknown to me – I am glad it is so – whether I have a long spell of service or not, whether by life or by death, I want to glorify the Lord Jesus in my body and live a 100 per cent life for Him and lost souls."

For six weeks he tried to show the love of God to the Lobis by treating their illnesses as best he could but it all came to an abrupt end on the evening of 20ᵗʰ March. Extracts from Jack Robertson's letter home tell what happened:

"A walk at dusk to get a breath of air...... a sudden pain in his left foot as though he had stepped upon a thorn....... The return to the house......... the sight of the marks where two fangs of a snake had gone in.........cutting with a scalpel ....injections..........the visits of the French Doctor from Gaoua......... the fight for his life.......... Haemorrhage external and internal...........

About 2:30 on Sunday morning he began to approach the gates of the Celestial City. His breathing became more pronounced until the last one came at 3:10 a.m. 20ᵗʰ March and he moved into the presence of the King of Kings. We laid his mortal remains to rest at Gaoua at 6 p.m. the same day."

Jack's letter went on to say;

"I think that nearly all the village called at the house wanting to see him. When the first folks asked, I was going to refuse them, but it came to me that he had given his life for the Lobis and therefore they had a right to see him. I was glad of this decision later as I was thrilled to see them round his bed. They were touched very much indeed – tears in the eyes of many of them."

Satan was fighting hard to retain his hold over the hearts and minds of the Lobi people. The work had been dogged by illness and death and fierce opposition from powerful witchdoctors but God's Word would not return empty to Him and under the guidance of Jack Robertson and other W.E.C. missionaries, the Lobi Church would flourish and grow strong. Sam Staniford summed it up well when he said,

"The battle for the Lobis is costly, but it will be worthwhile."

22

TORPEDOED

The following year, the world was torn apart by the Second World War and missionary activity in many countries was greatly disrupted. Travel to and from Africa became almost impossible, so it was a matter of grave concern when Alice was advised to return from Nigeria to Northern Ireland in 1941, for the sake of her health. She had spent much of the previous four years in bed with fevers, trying to carry on her work among the women from her sickbed, with the help of a young Christian boy. It eventually became too much for her and they began to make plans for her return.

It was extremely difficult to know what to do, as they constantly heard news of ships being sunk in many places, particularly around the west coast of Africa. They learnt that eighty percent of the ships belonging to Elder Dempster's had been lost. They prayed about the situation and booked a passage.

Both of them confessed to sensing that "that something would happen on the way", but they were convinced that it was the Lord's time for Alice to go home. She was travelling with one of the other missionaries and they prayed specifically that the Lord would give Alice the right cabin and that He would take care of all her baggage.

The two ladies set off for Lagos, where they spent the Christmas of 1941 waiting for a boat. They eventually got on board the William Wilberforce, a small cargo vessel, with room for twelve passengers. The purser met them with the words,

"This is your cabin, but there's a better cabin on the other side."

"Is this the cabin we were appointed to?" enquired Alice.

"Yes," replied the purser.

"Then we'll take that one, because we prayed that we might be given the right cabin."

The ship set sail and a day out from Sierra Leone, the captain opened his sealed orders – he had instructions to sail straight to New York! Soon the two ladies found themselves far out into the Atlantic.

Alice took fever and was lying on her bunk in her nightgown one evening. She was feeling too ill to go into dinner but the other passengers were standing in the upstairs alleyway, waiting for the dining room to open at 7 o'clock. Suddenly there was a terrific explosion – the ship had been torpedoed! The lights all went out and the passengers were left stumbling about in the darkness of a tropical night.

Without knowing how she got there, Alice found herself in a lifeboat. She learnt later that the torpedo had struck on the side of the ship where the purser had offered to give her the alternative cabin. That cabin was submerged in the water and the young man who occupied it only escaped by smashing his way out of the cabin with a heavy metal box. Had Alice accepted the change of cabin, it is unlikely that she would have survived.

Her ordeal wasn't over, however, and Alice would testify later on that she had never realised the nearness of the Lord so very definitely as she had done at that time. They spent six days and five nights in the lifeboat in the middle of the Atlantic – a dreadful ordeal especially for Alice and the two other ladies who had to contend with living in the embarrassingly close company of strange men. The sailors were good to her – lending her a pair of shorts and a pair of shoes – and somehow Alice managed to survive the experience.

They were miraculously picked up by an onion ship. The ship's usual route brought it round the north of the Canary Islands but on this occasion, it "happened" to travel round the south of the islands and intercepted the little lifeboat.

Stanley knew nothing of this drama until he received a cable, which read:

"BENINGTON AND BLUCK LANDED. ALL SAFE."

He rightly assumed that the wording meant that the ship had been torpedoed and praised God that the two ladies were safe. Because of the problems of communication during the war, it was three long months before he heard the whole story from Alice and could appreciate the full extent of her miraculous escape.

Stanley and Alice continued to serve God in Nigeria for the next ten years until they were forced to return home through ill health. Alice had battled with illness for many years and Stanley then began to experience problems with his eyes and also with his heart. In 1952, he was admitted to the Opthalmic Hospital in Great Victoria Street in Belfast and various tests were done. The news wasn't good. In a letter to Jean Corbett, a close friend and prayer partner, he wrote of his reaction to the test results:

"I have been moved into a ward where I am alone. The Lord's own loving thoughtfulness – though the Sisters take the credit for it! – that I may have quiet to think over the specialists' findings (again, His dear findings)

The heart specialist and the expert pathologist have both arrived, independently, at the decision that I should not go back to Africa! The eye specialists think the same about the eye condition, which they say is definitely due to my life and the work in Qua Iboe. So you will understand that such decisions will mean time for me to re-orientate myself......

The team of heart specialists recommend me to live in a bungalow and take it very easy for some time. (If they had stopped at 'bungalow', I could have returned to the Bible College – but the latter half precludes life as 'manager of schools'. How I would have loved it!) But He has assured us time and time again, in the past as well as now, that 'He will give thee much more than this' and 'your Heavenly Father knoweth what things ye have need of, before ye ask Him'.

Alice added her own footnote at the end of the letter:

"These past weeks have been a wonderful experience, and it has been a daily miracle to witness contentment and resignation to God's will in Stanley, lying blindfolded and inactive. I believe God has used this for His own glory."

So the next few years passed in comparative peace and quiet as they settled down once more to life in Northern Ireland. Stanley recovered his full health and strength and even Alice gained a measure of good health. They continued their close association with the Qua Iboe Mission and Stanley was able to help with translation work in the Efik language while he recuperated.

But slowly, surely, a surprising conviction was growing within their hearts. They knew they could not return to the rigours of full time work in Nigeria.............. but what about a little "gentle" translation work in that other land that was so dear to their hearts? Stanley couldn't ignore the conviction in his heart and in a letter to Jean, dated 27th May 1955, enthusiastically outlined the plans he had been making.

"I think," he reminded her, "that you have heard me more than once, say how I'd love to go back to the Lobi and finish the translation of the Lobi New Testament? Well, we now feel that this is the Lord's will for us. And, both of us have been passed by our own Doctor (who knows the worst about us – physically!) to return.

Well I felt for months past that I should do this Wycliffe Language Course and now that we have this recall from the Lord, I sent in my application, was accepted and go to London from 3rd July to 16th September. I want the language just upon the right basis from the restart of work upon it. They give a thorough grounding in the making up of a grammar, preparation of literacy campaign material, building of vocabulary and translation work.

I spoke to Isaac about it and he was against the project...........Next I went to JK (Wallace) and put the matter to him............. I think he thinks I'm crackers as I would have no one behind me...............

I know of course that there will be great difficulties and some hardships but that's not exactly a new state of affairs for us. We feel that to be allowed to even put the work of translation on the move along the right lines, if we cannot finish it, would be well worthwhile.

I have written to the NBSS (National Bible Society of Scotland) and they seemed to be interested, but how much help they can give I do not know."

The letter went on to say that despite not knowing exactly where their support would come from, they had already begun to make preparations for their return and had even booked passages for the end of October.

Now they felt they could make some sense of their enforced return from Nigeria and the fact that they were still considered unfit to even carry out relief work in that land. They sensed that the Lord had more important work in mind for them – the completion of the Lobi New Testament.

Two things confirmed their call – the Scottish Bible society agreed to fund them and while Stanley was in Scotland seeking their sponsorship, Alice received from the Lord a very personal commission which would encourage and sustain her through the trials and difficulties that lay ahead.

13

BACK IN BOUROUM-BOUROUM

They returned in 1956 to Bouroum-Bouroum, a village that, in some respects at least, had hardly changed at all. The narrow paths still wound through farms of millet, the people still lived in mud block houses, though here and there a corrugated iron roof gleamed in the sunlight. The little village boys still looked after the animals and the market stalls sold the same food. The men continued to farm their land with a "daba" (a type of wood and metal hoe) and anxiously looked to the sky for the rain to bring a good harvest.

In other respects, it was like a new world. Where once Stanley's bicycle had attracted a crowd of envious onlookers, now many of the villagers owned their own bicycles. Where once his car had been the only vehicle and he had difficulties getting petrol for it, now pick up trucks were a common sight, bringing supplies into the market and transporting people from place to place. Every so often a huge grader was sent down the main roads to "iron out" the bumps, making the long journeys much more comfortable until the next time the rains tore deep ruts into the laterite. A white refrigerator stood in the corner of the mission house and the mail was delivered by aeroplane!

They shared the mission house with Jack Robertson and his wife, who had continued to serve the Lord in Bouroum-Bouroum in the intervening years. The house was bigger than before, and was divided into two attached dwellings for the two couples. The grass roof had been replaced with a corrugated iron roof and plywood ceilings had been put in to keep the rooms cooler. Mosquito netting covered the window frames and corrugated iron shutters were hinged at the top to provide extra shade from the sun or protection from the storms.

Soon Stanley and Alice (or Ben and MaBen, as they were affectionately known to their colleagues) established a routine for their day. Alice was quite frail and spent most of the day in the house, trying to keep cool behind the grass mats they had hung at the windows. Although life wasn't easy for her, she was never heard to complain and impressed all who knew her by the gracious way she endured the hardships of life in Lobiland. She welcomed visitors to her home and tried to encourage Stanley in the translation work.

Stanley rose each day soon after 4 a.m. and always had his Bible reading, prayer and physical exercise before most other people were awake. He shaved by candlelight and then he and Alice had their regular breakfast of porridge. This meant that he could be at his desk by 6 a.m. and so begin work while it was still fairly cool. Brian Woodford, who joined the W.E.C. team in 1959, was very impressed, on one occasion when he had to go through Bouroum-Bouroum at about six o'clock in the morning, to see Stanley waiting to greet him at the double entrance gates into the compound, neatly dressed in well-pressed shorts and shirt, hair brushed and freshly shaved at a time when most other missionaries were still in bed.

Brian was stationed at Malba, as the pioneer missionary among the Birifor people and was intrigued by the story of how the work had begun there. During Stanley's early years, he had visited Malba, a village about fifty kilometres from Bouroum-Bouroum, and a Birifor man called Samba received Christ. Stanley described what had happened in a letter he wrote the next day, after spending the night in the Malba Government rest house.

"Samba invited me to go to his mud house and we knelt there on the flat mud roof, under the stars, while Samba prayed. It was so real that it was as if I could hear the angels singing up in heaven."

There were no other converts in the village and for the next twenty years, Samba stood alone, enduring constant persecution. Apart from the occasional visit from Jack Robertson, he had no fellowship and after he had been converted for four years, he began to pray that God would send a missionary to his people. Brian Woodford arrived sixteen years later and realised that exactly sixteen years earlier, when he was only ten, God had first called him to be a missionary in Africa. He often wondered if that was the first day Samba had prayed and praised God for yet another example of His wonderful timing.

It wasn't easy for Stanley to switch from the Ibibio language that he had been using for the past fifteen years, so it was vital to have someone to help him. He decided to engage the help of Dakprou, a man whom he had known in the earlier years. Dakprou had burnt his idols and had seemed to be following the Lord but, during the period of Stanley's absence, Dakprou's father had died and he had been handed the family idols to look after. Sadly, he had gone back to the old ways.

He was still happy, however, to spend time talking to Stanley about Lobi customs, helping him with the language and discussing the translation work.

Later another young Christian man, Jean Senkpe, came to help too and many hours were spent in discussion about the best way to translate the often difficult concepts of God's Word. Sometimes they had just no idea what to write and, at those moments, Stanley would simply drop to his knees and pray, trusting that God Himself would enlighten their minds.

One of the most challenging passages was the twenty third Psalm and, some years later, Stanley would describe the problems they faced:

"The Lord – what are we going to put for 'Lord'? There is no Lord in Lobi land. There are no chiefs and everyone is a law unto himself, so what can we use for 'Lord'? What is 'Lord' anyway? It's a name, the Name Jehovah – we'll start off with that!"

"The Lord is my Shepherd............. My Shepherd – what does that mean? That means a man who looks after my sheep, doesn't it?.......... Now that won't do, because that would mean that the Lord was a little boy with a long stick who beats the sheep and the cows and the goats to keep them out of the crops............."
Stanley puzzled over this for quite some time. He knew the idea that he wanted to get across – he knew what it meant to him for the Lord to be his Shepherd.

"He is the One who takes me in His arms when I'm not able to walk myself, when I'm not able to follow the herd, when I get behind," he thought. "He takes me up in His arms and carries me. If I stray from the path, He's after me........... The Lord is my Shepherd and everything will be all right because He is my Shepherd................."

"I can't say that the Lord is a little boy who races his sheep against other boys' sheep to see whose sheep can run the fastest; who rides on the cows and treats them badly."

The solution came to him on one of his visits to a nearby village where he met with the Christians every Sunday and Wednesday. On Sundays he would read to them what he had translated that week and on Wednesdays, he would hold literacy classes and pray with them. During one of the prayer times, one Godly Christian man stood up to pray.

"Oh Lord," he said, "Thou art the cowbird that cares for me."

"That's it," thought Stanley excitedly, "that's the word to use for Shepherd!"

The cowbird travels with the cattle and flies up into the air, beating his wings and squawking loudly if there is any danger. The bird sits on the backs of the cows and picks out anything on its skin that might be bothering it – the cowbird looks after the cows! That is what the Shepherd is – He looks after the sheep Himself. He is not the person we employ to look after the sheep!

His next problem was the translation of the words "green pastures". Stanley knew the image that came to his mind when he read those words:

"I see a lovely little stream murmuring its way through a meadow," he mused, "with willow trees hanging over the water and birds singing in the branches and cows lying down in the shade, contentedly chewing the cud. There is nothing like that in Lobi land."

He discussed the concept of the green pastures with Dakprou, but he couldn't give him a word that would satisfactorily express the meaning. Then Stanley remembered something that he had seen many times at the end of the dry season. The Lobis would set fire to the tall elephant grass to clear the ground for planting the crops again. Large areas of the countryside would be completely burnt and Stanley had often noticed that, just a few days afterwards, little tender shoots of grass would spring up in every clump of burnt grass. This was the grass the animals all liked best – new and sweet and juicy – and that was the word he would use for 'green pastures'.

One day in the middle of their work, Dakprou asked Stanley, "Douda, can I get a drink of water, it's over there?"

He had to go behind Stanley to fetch the water and as he returned to his chair, he said,

"Excuse me for going behind you."

Stanley looked at him in some surprise – at home it was considered impolite to walk in front of someone but Dakprou wanted to be excused for walking behind him!

Dakprou explained that he excused himself "because I might have tramped on your shadow."

"What would that do?" enquired Stanley.

"It might bring you sickness or kill you."

Stanley listened with interest as Dakprou went on.

"If a man has done something which displeases you and you're angry with him, you watch when he's in the marketplace, or on the road and you see where his shadow has fallen and you stoop down quickly and pick up a handful of sand. You take that to the witchdoctor and very soon you will have that man on his back, because the shadow is the second life of a man."

Suddenly Stanley began to realise that this Lobi belief might have implications for the translation of another phrase in the Psalm – 'the valley of the shadow of death'. To save any confusion, he simply translated the phrase 'the valley of the darkness of death'.

And so the work went on, slowly, painstakingly, phrase by phrase, verse by verse, chapter by chapter, through the Gospels, through the New Testament letters.

He developed a great relationship with young Jean Senkpe and taught him to read and also to preach. Jean was much impressed by Stanley's neatness and meticulous attention to detail. Everything had to be put away tidily each evening after they finished the work. When Jean enquired why this had to be done, Stanley told him,

"So that when Jesus comes, people will know I was a tidy person!"

The two men concentrated much of their efforts on the village of Djegona, where a little group of believers had formed a church. As he watched the young man grow in his faith and develop a passion for evangelism and for the Word of God, he realised his potential for the future.

"One day," Stanley told him, "you will be a Pastor among the Lobis. I'm going to put money aside for you to go to Bible School."

His words were prophetic for Jean not only went to Bible School as a student, but in later years went on to become the head of the Lobi Bible School in Bouroum-Bouroum. One of Stanley's final acts before he died was to check with Mady Vaillant that she had sent money for Jean's support. He used to call Jean "the jewel in my crown".

24

FINAL SCENES

Stanley had always taken a great interest in photography and had set up a type of darkroom in his house in the early days. He took some really good black and white photographs of the Lobi people during his first stay in Bouroum-Bouroum but when he returned in the fifties, he was the proud owner of a cine camera. How exciting it was to be able to take "moving pictures" of the places and the people he had come to love and what a joy it would be to be able to show the folks back home just what life was really like.

The Super 8 films were later edited and made in to an amateur video which provided a fascinating insight into the Church life and the customs of the people. He chronicled the procession of the children from Bouroum-Bouroum walking in single file to the initiation ceremony and brought his camera to the market place to film them when they returned, the boys in their feather headgear and all of them wearing costumes made from strings of cowrie shells.

He paid his respects at a Lobi funeral, where he was allowed to film the eerie "questioning of the corpse" and the endless dancing and the sacrifices that were made.

In contrast to these somewhat sad scenes, he was delighted to tape the burning of the idols of the first Christian in Ntodjara, and some of the scenes at a Church conference at Djegona. Other W.E.C. missionaries had joined them on the compound by this time and he took an impish pleasure in capturing Mady Vaillant and Greti Oesch on their motorbikes or giving out medicines or walking into the little house that had been built for them.

These two young missionaries grew to love and respect 'Ben' and 'MaBen' for the older couple were a great encouragement to them both, Before Greti arrived, Mady was grateful for the little visits Stanley used to make, usually about four o'clock in the afternoon, just to see where she had got to in her language study. He would talk for a little while and pray with her, asking God to give her 'a quick mind, a ready tongue and a retentive memory'.

The exploits of a young Dutch missionary featured on the film too. He helped to dig out a new well for the compound at Bouroum-Bouroum and very bravely climbed down into its depths, only to find Stanley's camera trained on him as he re-emerged. Not even the Beningtons' cat escaped the film maker – it was shot capturing an iguana for its tea.

When Stanley's niece, Yvonne and her husband Andre, paid a visit to Bouroum-Bouroum in 1962, they too featured on screen. Their visit was made possible because Andre was undertaking research into the languages of Northern Ghana for the University of Ghana and was able to carry out some of his research in the Bouroum-Bouroum area, as Lobiri was part of the Voltaic languages, spoken in Upper Volta and Northern Ghana.

Their visit was a mutual blessing to both couples. Andre was able to assist Stanley with the Lobi grammar he was working on and also to help Mady with her language study, though he suspected that Mady was just a little in awe of this "linguistic expert" who had come to visit!

Yvonne enjoyed being with her fun-loving Uncle Stanley again and appreciated the efforts Alice made to make them feel at home, efforts that included the making of Lobi ice cream from guinea fowl eggs, condensed milk and mangoes – delicious! She smiled too at

Stanley's sly method of getting second helpings served up. He would tell Alice,

"Now don't keep Andre waiting for another portion of ice cream!"
Yvonne and Andre saw the Benington "faith in action" on the very first night in Bouroum-Bouroum. When they arrived, Alice was down to the last twelve bottles of water in the fridge – not nearly enough for the four of them. They weren't concerned, however, and just prayed that the rain would come. It did – that very night there was a storm and the first good rain of the season fell.

They were also impressed by the disciplined lifestyle of their uncle and aunt and their ready obedience to the will of God. They often walked past the office where Stanley worked and saw his head bowed over the papers in front of him, the very epitome of dedication. They watched as the older couple went out for a walk together every evening, just at dusk, going as far as the first tree if Alice wasn't feeling too well, or to the second tree if she felt a little better. They would watch the nightly spectacle of the fruit bats, streaming overhead, many thousands of them heading for their favourite feeding places.

Mady sometimes accompanied them and she was often amused by the typical conversation Stanley would have with the Lobi men, who at that time were returning from their day's work in the fields.

"Where are you going?" they would ask Stanley.

"We walk for nothing," Stanley would reply, smiling at the look on the face of the questioner who always found it hard to understand why someone would want to walk for "nothing".

Everyday scenes from the village, captured by Stanley on his cine camera, brought to life the details he had written about in his letters home: the Lobi women walking long distances to the marsh to find water during the dry season; men making their way to the fields, carrying calabashes of Lobi beer; children playing a game of chance with cowrie shells; similar shells, still used as currency, being counted by the Church treasurer; the Robertsons' little girl busily grinding millet between two stones to make flour, while her Lobi friend pounded more millet in a mortar; four children gathered round one calabash of water, vainly trying to take a bath in the dry season; a little baby fast asleep in a Lobi basket; a blind man playing the balaphone (an instrument rather like a xylophone).

The longest coverage was given to the scenes that were dearest to his heart – there are many shots of the literacy classes, little circles of children, sitting on the sand, faces alight with the sheer pleasure of being able to interpret the words on the page. The arrival of booklets from the Scripture Gift Mission was well documented. Stanley filmed the package just after it arrived, then Jean, his co-translator, was given the honour of opening the parcel in the village of Djegona. A little group of children gathered round and Jean distributed the booklets. Neither Stanley nor Jean had any way of knowing it at that time, but for one of those little boys who received a booklet that day, it was the beginning of a journey in education that would see him being the first in his family to go to school. Little Timothy would later study medicine in Niger, Ivory Coast and France, eventually qualifying as a surgeon.

There were also many Church scenes – most of them filmed in Djegona.

Stanley attended a Church conference there, before he and Alice left for home again and enjoyed so much watching Christians from as far away as Gaoua meeting together to worship God and sing His praises.

Stanley had always enjoyed singing and in his early days among the Lobis, had attempted to write hymns for them to sing. Since the Lobi language didn't have words like 'repent' or 'glory' or 'grace', Stanley had to resort to stringing together lots of words to try and express these concepts. These long strings of words didn't sing too well and the matter was further complicated by the fact that Lobi was a tonal language, so when a tune was put to the words, it usually made the words meaningless! The people did their best but it was obvious to Stanley's helper, Jean, that it was a real struggle for them.

He decided to do something about it and composed one or two Lobi songs himself and introduced them to the Church at Djegona. He was dismayed to find that the elders were very upset and refused to sing these new songs.

"But why?" asked a bewildered Jean.

"It is clearly wrong to sing anything that makes sense, because Dauda always taught us to sing songs that don't mean anything," they replied!

Fortunately Jean was able to persuade them that it might be a good idea for their praise to make sense and from then on, the singing improved dramatically.

The other Church that featured regularly on the filming was the Church at Bouroum-Bouroum. When he had returned to the village, he had been saddened by the small numbers who attended the little, long, narrow church that had been built across the road from the mission compound. There were still so few attending when Brian Woodford arrived, that he found it difficult to understand why this man, who had a weak heart and sight in only one eye, would come out of 'retirement' to spend years translating the New Testament for so few believers. Brian asked Stanley about it one day and so Stanley told him the story of the promise God had given him of three thousand converts.

"I'm translating the Bible for the Church I know will come into being," he had said.

It was slow work and in later years Jack Robertson would refer to the fruit among the Lobis as being 'handpicked, requiring an abundance of patience and perseverance'.

So it was with great delight that Stanley brought his camera to the service one day and panned along the faces of seven of the members, many of whom were sons of the very first believers among the Lobi people. One of Tigite's sons was there, son of the one in whose dreams he had walked all those years ago. David and Thomas were there, both of them serving the Lobi Church at that very time. Andre, who in later years would become one of the well respected Church leaders, who would help with the on going translation work and teach in the Lobi Bible School, was there. The past, the present and the future of the work so dear to the hearts of Stanley and Alice – all represented in that group of young men.

Shortly after those scenes were shot, Stanley and Alice left Bouroum-Bouroum for the last time. By that stage, Alice was so ill with what had been discovered to be Tuberculosis that they found it almost impossible to find an airline willing to allow her to travel home, because of the risk to other passengers. But the God who had called them there and who had sustained them during this last supreme effort, proved Himself to be faithful in all things, even to arranging their passage with an Italian airline.

As the plane carried them swiftly from the airport at Ougadougou, across the mighty Sahara Desert, over the Mediterranean Sea and journeyed on above the continent of Europe, Stanley and Alice looked forward with joy to being home once again and also to the day when they would hear the news that the translation of the New Testament, on which Stanley had worked so hard, was finally in the hands of his beloved Lobi people.

And in their hearts, did they hear a gentle whisper, "Well done, good and faithful servants"? There is no doubt that, when they were finally ushered into the Presence of the Lord they had served so faithfully and so sacrificially, they did hear those words, not in a gentle whisper, but ringing out across Heaven in the mighty voice of the Master. And in later years, those left behind would do the calculations and marvel afresh at the faithful way our God keeps His promises. By the time Stanley died, the promise God had made to him at the beginning of the work had been fulfilled – every one of the three thousand Lobi converts promised to him in the place prepared for him, had been brought into the Kingdom.

Our God keeps His Word!

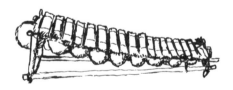

Rw
25/9/02

7LW
25/9/02

25

THE DAGARI STONE

For many years, W.E.C. International carried on the work in Upper Volta (or Burkina Faso, as it would later be named). The Lobi Church grew under the leadership of pastors and elders like Pastor Job and Pastor Jean. Other missionaries came to work among the Lobis and to revise and continue the translation of the Bible into Lobiri.

Meanwhile, the Qua Iboe Mission concentrated its efforts in Nigeria and a strong self-governing Church developed. Bible Colleges were formed and other areas of ministry were begun. By the late 1980s, however, the General Secretary, Rev. Bill Leach, and some of the Council members had become concerned about the decline in the number of missionaries working in the country. For various reasons, quite a few missionaries had to return home and there were few new candidates to replace them.

Around the same time, one of the Council members, Graham Cheesman, who had recently returned from a period of service in one of the Qua Iboe Bible Colleges, was greatly challenged by an article in "Christianity Today". The article, written by Donald A McGavran, claimed that many missionary societies had become "chained" to the Churches they had helped to form and asserted that missions needed to break the links and go back to the task of evangelising unreached people groups.

Bill and Graham met for lunch and discussed these issues. Bill expressed his conviction that the mission should begin to look outside Nigeria, perhaps in another African country. As they continued talking, they realised that God had been leading them in a similar direction. Bill suggested that they should contact Patrick Johnstone, who was renowned for his extensive knowledge of world needs and for his compilation of the prayer guide, 'Operation World'.

Not long afterwards, Bill had to phone Patrick, in connection with Qua Iboe's Centenary preparations, to check some details about the Lobi people. Patrick told him that he had visited Burkina Faso recently and had in fact been telling his students that very morning about Stanley Benington and his work.

"He is a wonderful example to us all," he said and went on to inform Bill that the Lobi Church had recently sent out its first missionaries.

"Why don't you go back into Burkina Faso?" Patrick suggested, when Bill told him of the renewed vision God was giving the mission. He reminded Bill that the Qua Iboe Mission had worked there before and thought it made good sense to at least explore the possibility of renewing the association with W.E.C. He also suggested that the Mission might consider a new venture among the Dagari people.

When Bill brought this suggestion to the Council, it was agreed that a survey of Burkina Faso should be undertaken and Graham Cheesman was asked if he would be prepared to carry out this task. It was also agreed that, since Qua Iboe had always been primarily interested in reaching the unevangelised, they would not return to work among the Lobis. The members of the Council decided to take up Patrick's suggestion and so the survey was limited to the Southern Dagari people.

Graham arrived in Burkina Faso on 19th February 1990. He was warmly welcomed by the W.E.C. missionaries and greatly appreciated the help given to him by Walter and Suzanne Roesti and Mady Vaillant. He visited the mission compounds at Bouroum-Bouroum and Gaoua, gathering useful information from the missionaries working in those places. His survey then took him south to the village of Legmoin and two other Dagari villages and then right across to the bank of the Volta Noir river.

He was greatly impressed by the huge idol houses and the hut walls that were daubed with various symbols in an attempt to protect the owners from evil spirits. He saw great physical and spiritual needs, which were underlined for him on his visit to the river.

There was quite a lot of activity on the riverbank that day and Graham walked up on to a little hill nearby to get a better view. This caused some consternation among the people and they motioned to him and shouted at him to come down. He realised afterwards that they had been making preparations for a sacrifice on the hill and they didn't want him to be there.

That visible reminder of their spiritual needs remained with him for some time afterwards, as did the realisation that the boatman who waited at the edge of the river was blind, typifying the many medical needs that were apparent even to a non-medical observer.

At one point in his tour of the area, he came across an unusual stone, a lovely piece of white quartz. He picked it up and, on his return to Northern Ireland, gave it to Bill.

"There is a stone from Dagari land," he said. "Bring it back when you visit the first Qua Iboe Missionaries to the Dagaris!"

Bill was greatly taken with the Dagari stone and after the mission had decided to take a step of faith and return to Burkina Faso, he used to bring it with him on deputation visits.

"Many people who live in the place where this stone comes from have never heard of Jesus," he would tell his listeners. "Will you answer the call of God to the Dagaris?"

Unfortunately, no one answered the call in the years that followed and when Bill did have his only opportunity to visit the field in 1992, there were no missionaries to whom he could bring the stone. The lack of response to the need was a source of disappointment for Bill and the members of Council. Had they made a mistake? Would no one respond to the call?

They weren't to know, of course, but during those years of waiting, God was preparing the hearts of two young people. At the time of Graham's survey, they hadn't even met and neither of them had any intention of serving God in Burkina Faso. They couldn't foresee that one day, they would stand in Catherine Leach's home and hold the Dagari stone in their hands and hear the story of how it came to sit on the mantelpiece and realise that they were the answer to the prayers of many in the Qua Iboe family.

26

BROKEN ENGAGEMENT

It was unusual reading for a fourteen year old – the New Internationalist Magazine – but Jeremy found the issue on Upper Volta fascinating. As he read the details of far-away African people groups, he determined that one day he would go there as an aid worker. Although he would have considered himself to be a Christian because he attended the local Anglican Church in Welwyn, North London, his concern was not for their spiritual well being, but for their social needs. The idea that one day he might be a missionary never occurred to him.

A youth weekend organised by his local church and taken by students from Cambridge University, was to change not only his ideas about overseas service, but also his whole life. The challenge was thrown out,

"Put up your hands if you're a Christian."

When Jeremy and many others put up their hands, they were asked why they had done so. Jeremy's reply was confident,

"Because I go to church every Sunday."

The rest of the weekend was spent in discussion and study as the group sought to discover if there was more to being a Christian than mere church attendance. By the end of the weekend, Jeremy knew that he wasn't a Christian and he began to read the Bible. As his interest grew, he organised a trip to Greenbelt, a Christian music festival. He was surprised by the atmosphere – everyone seemed to be smiling. He enjoyed the music and was challenged by the messages delivered at the various sessions. Eventually he responded to one such message by going to the front of the tent where he was given a "Journey Into Life" booklet. From this simple beginning, his spiritual life grew until even his mother noticed that he had changed,

"Jeremy, you're different," she remarked one day, "you used to be such an angry young man. You've lost the chip on your shoulder."

At University in Newcastle, where he studied Geophysics, he met Tim, a young Christian student who brought him to church and became something of a mentor to him. They used to meet at lunchtime to pray, using "Operation World" to provide prayer topics and information.

He also became involved in Navigators, where he was encouraged to study the Bible and to witness, with the result that some of his student friends became Christians. He soon began to realize that people's spiritual needs were more important than their social needs and the focus of his desire to work overseas changed – he now wanted to serve as a missionary. Involvement with Beach Missions and Camps fuelled this desire, as did the thrilling stories he read of former missionaries, such as Hudson Taylor, C.T.Studd and James O. Fraser.

His degree and teacher training finished, Jeremy taught for three years in an English comprehensive school, Haydon Comprehensive. It was there he met Angie. She was an R.E. teacher in the school and they soon became friendly. They began seeing each other and it wasn't long before Jeremy realized that their friendship was beginning to blossom into something more serious. He knew that it was important that Angie understood about God's call on his life so, over a meal one day, he said,

"I think you should know – God's calling me to be a missionary."

Angie assured him that it was wasn't a problem to her, though she was honest enough to admit that she had not ever felt any such call on her own life. The matter was left there and over the next few months they grew closer together. Jeremy proposed and they got engaged in the June of his second year at the school. A wedding date was set for the following August, arrangements were made and the honeymoon was booked.

Gradually, however, Jeremy began to be troubled by a niggling sense of disquiet, which was brought to a head on a train journey to London. He and the friend with whom he was travelling were chatting together when his friend turned to him and asked,

"Are you really at peace about being married?"

Jeremy looked at him in some surprise but as he struggled for an answer, he recognised the significance of the moment and finally acknowledged that he was not completely at peace about the situation.

He determined to set aside a month in which to seek the Lord for an answer, praying that God would speak to him clearly and that he would be strong enough to obey the voice of God, whether the answer he received was the one he wanted to hear or not. He kept a note of his quiet times with God for that month.

It was to be one of the most difficult months of his life. He continued to see Angie and was reminded each time that he loved her. He watched her happily making wedding plans, knowing that he might well have to ruin her plans and take away her happiness.

"Lord, how can I do this?" he asked. "How will I ever be able to tell her that the wedding is off? You will have to make it very clear if Your answer is no!"

In the middle of the month, he and Angie went to a weekend for engaged couples, run by Joyce Huggett. Jeremy was greatly disturbed by a comment made at that weekend,

"When you start married life, it's like knocking down old walls and starting afresh."

Although he could understand the truth in the statement, he identified the old walls in his life with his strong sense of calling to the mission field and knew that there was no way that these walls could be knocked down. Somehow he got through the rest of the weekend but when Monday morning came, he felt so ill that he was unable to go to school. The next few days passed in a haze of sickness and worry but still he felt he had no answer from God.

He then set aside three days to fast and pray but even at the end of that time he had not heard God's voice. In a somewhat desperate attempt to take his mind off the situation, he went to visit two of his friends, Richard and Angie. They spent a little while just talking but Jeremy couldn't keep up the pretence that all was well and he burst into tears. In response to their immediate concern, he told them a little about his dilemma and then went back to his own house feeling calmer.

That night he woke up at four o'clock and in a strange way knew that he would not be going back to sleep because God was going to speak to him. He reached for his Bible, intending to look for verses about having the courage to do what is right, but as he opened the New Testament, his eyes fell on to the middle of the page containing 1Corinthians chapter 7 and he read the words of verse 32.

"It is better for me to remain single."

That was it! He slept no more but spent the hours before dawn trying to come to terms with the idea that his engagement was over and also trying to prepare himself for the awful task that lay ahead of him – breaking the news to Angie.

Next day was a training day for the teachers at the school and Jeremy kept having to find a quiet place to let the tears flow as the realisation of what he had to do just overwhelmed him. He drove to Angie's house after school but, before going in, he went round the block of houses, praying and thinking about the best way to break the news. There was no easy way to do it and eventually he just said,

"Listen Angie, I've been praying about this for a month now….." and explained what had happened.

Angie was shocked – totally unprepared for the news Jeremy had brought.

"I need to have someone here with me. Do you mind if I phone my Pastor?"

He arrived very quickly and his advice was wise but difficult to carry out - "Don't say anything to anyone for two weeks."

Those two weeks took on a surreal quality. To all those around them, nothing had changed. They were still an engaged couple, happily planning for a wedding and a future life together. Only they knew the truth and as the days went by it became harder to keep up the pretence. Yet in the midst of it all, Jeremy knew the peace of God in his heart.

They told both sets of parents what was happening and at the end of the two weeks, Jeremy went back to the minister, sure that it was the will of God for the marriage to be called off. Angie went into the room afterwards and Jeremy made his way home. That night the enormity of what he had done pressed in upon him and he cried for Angie and the hurt he knew she must be feeling. He cried too for himself and the shattering of cherished hopes and dreams.

There followed a long, difficult period for both of them. They were still teaching in the same school and saw each other every day. Jeremy had already begun applying to various Bible Colleges but despite having had no definite reply to his enquiries, he decided to resign from the school.

As he wrote his letter of resignation, he was very aware that he was closing one chapter in his life and he wondered what God might have in store for him – somewhere there was a place prepared for him and he was trusting God to lead him to it.

27

RACHEL

Jeremy picked up the letter with the All Nations Bible College logo on the front and opened it eagerly. Yes, he had been given an interview. The next phase of his life was about to begin. His vision to serve the men and women he had read about all those years ago would soon be fulfilled – just a few years at Bible College lay in between.

When the time came, he set off for the interview, well prepared and very confident. As the interview progressed, however, his confidence waned and he became ill at ease. Something didn't feel right. His suspicions were confirmed when the interviewing panel informed him that they would not accept him for the course at that time but suggested that he should gain some short-term experience first. Although initially disappointed by their decision, he decided to accept it as God's decision and wrote to a number of missionary societies enquiring about short-term service. Eventually he was offered a short-term placement with W.E.C. International and set off in September for the Bourafaye Mission School in Senegal.

The next two years were busy, exciting and fulfilling. Jeremy taught Science, Mathematics and Art to missionary children and thoroughly enjoyed the experience of being in Africa – the warm climate, the laid-back attitude to life, the different culture..... Although he enjoyed it, he knew that it wasn't the place prepared for him. His heart was still set on the country he had read about all those years ago – now renamed Burkina Faso. He would not know until some years later that this period in his life was to be a wonderful preparation for what lay ahead, particularly in the light of the partnership between W.E.C. and Q.I.F. under which he would eventually work.

On returning home he applied once again to Bible college but this time he sent his application to Moorlands Bible College, near Bournemouth. He was accepted for the two year Missions Course but had little idea that God was planning to provide not only necessary training for his future work, but also a wife!

Rachel quite literally "walked" into Jeremy's life at the beginning of his second year. On the first Sunday of the new term a walk had been organised to help integrate the new students and Jeremy found himself walking along beside one of the freshers. Jeremy didn't realize that Rachel had already seen him at a social evening, had been attracted by his "lovely eyes" and had idly wondered if he was married!

"And where have you come from?" he asked.

"I've been working in Kenya for the past four and a half years and I'm hoping to go out there again with the Africa Inland Mission."

Jeremy was surprised by the sense of disappointment that he felt on hearing this news!

"Oh well, that wouldn't work then," he thought.

They found it easy to talk to each other and that Sunday afternoon walk was the beginning of a very special friendship.

Rachel grew up in the suburbs of London and became a Christian at the age of fourteen, during a Confirmation class. She had no early sense of calling to missionary work. On the contrary, she was startled by the suggestion made to her at a Youth Fellowship meeting. The young people were exploring what they thought those in the group might do later in life and someone said to Rachel,

"I think you will be a missionary."

"No way!" was her immediate response. Inspired by stories of life at boarding school, she asked her parents if they would send her to a boarding school about thirty miles from her home. They agreed, and so her sixth form years were spent at a mixed boarding school, which she thoroughly enjoyed. Before obtaining a degree in Geography from Durham University, Rachel took a year out. For five months, she lived with a family in the Solomon Islands, helping them with the two little girls. Returning home by plane would have been too tame for Rachel, who chose to make the journey (with a couple of friends) via the Trans Siberian Railway, having taken a boat to Russia from Hong Kong. The last leg of the journey entailed a memorable trip down through Scandanavia. This well developed sense of independence would prove to be very useful in later years!

She came to mission almost by "chance". She wanted to give something back to God in return for all that He had given to her. Added to that was the fact that her father had been born and raised in Kenya and she had a strong desire to go and see the land of her father's birth. Another link in the chain was an eight-month job with the Civil Service on completing her degree. She was standing at the photocopier one day, talking to a young man about her interest in Kenya, when he said that he knew an M.A.F. pilot working in Nairobi.

"I'll give you his address, if you like," he offered.

The pilot, Peter de Bourcier, was able to arrange a nine-month stay in Nairobi, working in the bookings office and helping with flight monitoring. She learnt a great deal about mission support and was introduced to the work of the Africa Inland Mission. When her time in Nairobi finished, Rachel spent eighteen months in Germany with Campus Crusade, after which she applied for a short-term placement back in Africa with A.I.M. The "short-term" turned out to be four and a half years! She enjoyed her work in the finance office of A.I.M. International Services and the experience she gained was invaluable – meeting many missionaries, being invited into bush situations and getting to know and love Africa.

In all of these situations, Rachel was aware that one of the main reasons for her frequent moves was to avoid having to undertake further study. She didn't enjoy studying and felt that she had done enough but God had other ideas! He knew that she had a divine appointment to keep - a special Sunday afternoon walk in a Bible college and so He dangled an irresistible carrot to bring her there.

"We've been asked to run the T.I.M.O. programme," the Director of Services told her, "and we'd like you to work with us."

T.I.M.O. (Training in Ministry Outreach) was an exciting new programme recently set up by A.I.M. to place new missionaries with more experienced missionaries in new locations among unchurched people groups. Rachel realised that if she wanted to be involved with it, she would have to apply to work full-time with the mission and Bible college training was one of the requirements. She began to pray about it and to ask people for advice because she had no idea where she should go.

"Why don't you go to Moorlands?" suggested two of her colleagues who had been there themselves, "it's a brilliant place."

Her mother had also found out about Moorlands and felt that it would suit Rachel very well so, accepting these suggestions as God's guidance, she applied to, and was accepted for, a one year course, little realising the profound effect that decision would have on her life.

28

ANOTHER PLACE PREPARED

As Jeremy's relationship with God developed, so did his understanding of what he calls God's "Kairos" – the amazing planning and timing of God which results in the bringing together of people or events in a particularly significant way. One such "Kairos" occurred when Jeremy began to plan for his college field term. Having enjoyed his short -term placement with W.E.C., he was interested in setting up his field term with the same mission, but this time in the country that God had put on his heart –no longer called Upper Volta, but Burkina Faso.

 With some of his fellow students, Jeremy attended the Annual Missionary Conference of the Evangelical Alliance and, as he looked around at those who were there, he realised that, by a wonderful miracle, God had brought together in the same place and at the same time, a busy Missions tutor, the W.E.C. candidate secretary, Jeremy and Phil, his Church missions secretary.

 "Can we get together to talk about this?" Jeremy asked them. They were able to discuss his placement on the spot and all agreed that he should take a look at other missions, particularly for long-term work. So began the search for another mission that worked in Burkina Faso.

He wondered about Africa Inland Mission, having listened to Rachel talk of her involvement with it. He was unable to come up with any other possibilities, so he wrote directly to the W.E.C. field leaders to ask if he could go out with them and his ten-week placement was confirmed. He was not to know just how significant that decision would be.

Before he even heard of the Qua Iboe Fellowship or knew anything of its history or its connection with Burkina Faso, Jeremy spent the first two weeks of his placement in Bouroum Bouroum, living in a house close to the site of the Beningtons' house! He was shown the concrete base of what had been Stanley's home and visited the graves of those who had died while on missionary service.

After spending two weeks in Bouroum Bouroum, Jeremy went to stay with a family in Sideradougou where he was involved in a week of evangelism with the Jesus film. As part of his field term he had to complete an 8,000 word dissertation on a people group, so he went to Gaoua to write it up. While in Gaoua, he "happened" to pick up a sheet of paper on which were details of the church's interest in beginning a new work with the Dagari people. It was a new outreach – rural church planting with tribal people. As he read on, he discovered that the associated mission was not to be W.E.C. but the Qua Iboe Fellowship. He felt in his heart an immediate response – a response so strong that he felt it as a physical lurching in his stomach. This was exactly the sort of work that Jeremy had been interested in for so long.

"Do you think it might be possible for me to visit Legmoin?" he asked Walter.

"Well that might be a bit awkward but I'll see if Fabian could take you - you don't mind travelling on a moped?"

So the following Sunday found Jeremy holding on tightly to the waist of a young French volunteer, a member of the W.E.C. team who had agreed to bring him to Legmoin. It was the end of the dry season and the one and a half hour journey along the bumpy laterite road was dusty and uncomfortable.

They arrived in time for church, which was held in a small building with mud walls and a thatched roof. There were about thirty people sitting on the low wooden benches. They looked up with interest when Jeremy was introduced and he felt at home among them.

During the service, a young man with a smiling face was brought to the front to be introduced to the people.

"This is Zougbile – he is our new Pastor. It is his first Sunday here in Legmoin."

Jeremy looked into Zougbile's face and wondered once again at God's amazing timing. How incredible that on the only Sunday when it was possible for Jeremy to be in Legmoin, the new Pastor should be commencing his ministry.

They had lunch together and, as they ate, Jeremy told Zougbile about his interest in working among the Dagari. Zougbile's eyes lit up and his smile grew even wider as he thought of the possibility of working in partnership with the young man who was sharing his lunch.

Somehow the return journey to Gaoua didn't seem quite so uncomfortable – Jeremy's mind was full of dreams and plans and the miles passed unnoticed. Surely this was the way forward – it all seemed so right. Maybe the next time he rode along this bumpy, dusty road it would be as a full-time missionary to the Dagari.

Just as Stanley's place in Bouroum-Bouroum had been prepared by God, so Jeremy would come to realise that the village of Legmoin had been prepared for him!

Many years earlier, one of Stanley's helpers, Juremiko, (or Papa Job, as he had become known) began to pray for an area south of Bouroum-Bouroum and Gaoua, which included the villages of Legmoin and Batie. His earnest prayer was echoed in the heart of Eileen Summerville, who had lived in Batie in the seventies and who had travelled on many occasions with an American couple to preach in Legmoin. Their contact in the village had been a Nigerian Christian who had opened his home for the services. There had been no response to the Gospel at that time and eventually the Nigerian couple left the village. Eileen continued to have a very real burden for the Batie and Legmoin areas. Such was her burden that her mission agreed to let her live alone in Batie. The work was discouraging as she saw little real fruit for her labour and eventually she settled in Gaoua.

She began to set aside a specific time each day to pray for God to move. When she shared the burden with the young pastor at Batie, Jean Baptiste, he and his wife joined her in prayer and soon God began to work.

It had been some years since anyone had really come to the Lord from Batie, so Eileen was surprised one day when a stranger came to her door and announced that he wanted to become a Christian.

"Tell me why," Eileen asked him.

Etienne explained that as a child he had attended Sunday School in the Batie Church but his father had been very unhappy about him doing so.

"This is the white man's religion," he had said and insisted that he must stop attending. In later life, he took on his father's idols.

"Recently," he told Eileen, "I have come to realise that I'm possessed by the spirits and I am frightened of becoming mad. I thought once more of Jesus and decided to go back to church. I knew that I should destroy my idols and today took some of them to the river. I threw them into the water but they jumped back out and stuck on my back. I tried again and this time I said the name of Jesus as I threw them in and they stayed there. So I want to follow Jesus."

"I need your help to destroy the other idols," he later told Eileen and the pastor. "They are very powerful and I want someone to help me."

Shortly afterwards, the whole church went to Etienne's house and prayed with him. He then destroyed his remaining idols, as almost everyone in his part of the village looked on in astonishment.

"You'll be dead in a month," the local witchdoctor announced, "and if the smoke touches those who are watching, they will die too."

His family and neighbours watched for that month and when Etienne didn't die, another man decided that he too would follow Jesus.

Eileen then suggested having a conference at Batie and the arrangements were made. Pastor Jean was invited to speak and the group decided to hold prayer meetings at 5am and 7pm each day of the week prior to the conference. God poured out His blessing on them and the people asked if the daily prayer meetings could continue. They agreed to hold one meeting each day and soon it was obvious that God had greatly increased their zeal for evangelism.

Further encouragement followed when another man from the Dagari people group brought his two wives to church one Tuesday night during the Prayer meeting. Francois had heard the singing and was curious to know what was going on. He trusted Jesus that night, along with his two wives. Eileen was delighted to discover that he had originally come from Legmoin.

Francois then shared the Gospel with his friend at the village of Bambassou and his friend also began to go to the church.

During one of the evening prayer meetings a Mossi lady had a vision which she shared with those who had gathered to pray.

"I saw a path that went in that direction," she told them, pointing towards Bambassou. " On the path I saw three upturned calabashes. I don't know what it means."

She turned to Eileen and asked, "Do you know what it means?"

Eileen had no idea either but they understood when they went to Francois' house to destroy his idols. Right in the middle of the idols, they saw three upturned calabashes and they recognised that the Lord was revealing His plan to open up a pathway to the work in Bambassou.

So the work grew, slowly, and several years went by. They began to use the Jesus film in many of the villages and were greatly encouraged when one Sunday a young Dagari fisherman arrived in the Batie church, saying that he had felt compelled to go there that day. The next Sunday, three other Dagaris came to the church, independently of each other and also confessed to experiencing the same inner conviction that they had to go to the church that day. All of them came from Bambassou and all of them gave their lives to the Lord, asking for the church to witness the burning of their idols.

The people in the village of Bambassou watched and declared that they would wait for two years to see if any harm came to them. Two years later, the Pastor of the Lobi church at Midebdo, Jean Ollo, was bitten by a snake and was brought to Batie hospital. He was sharing a room with Ouoro, a man from Bambassou, who had also been bitten. Ouoro watched with interest as the Christians from the Batie church came to pray for Jean Ollo and he too asked for prayer and became a Christian. They discovered that Ouoro was a powerful witchdoctor, the head of his household and when he became a Christian, twenty three others from his family also trusted in Jesus. God was building His church and preparing the place to which He planned to send Jeremy.

29

A BRIDE, A BABY AND BURKINA

There was a problem, of course – life is rarely simple, especially for those who are truly anxious to do God's will. Jeremy was fairly sure now that his future lay with the Dagari people in Burkina Faso but his relationship with a certain fair-haired student had become rather serious. Regular letters to and from Burkina had intensified their feelings and, on his return, they had begun to discuss the possibility of a long-term relationship.

The complication was, of course, that the purpose of Rachel's year at Moorlands was to prepare her for work with A.I.M. in an area thousands of miles away from Burkina Faso! She had already received her application forms and had begun to fill them in but was aware that there was little point in doing so if her relationship with Jeremy was serious. She prayed fervently that there would be clarity between what she was feeling and what God wanted. She was over thirty by now and would have liked to be married. On the other hand, she was worried about letting A.I.M. down and had been looking forward to working in the new placement.

After much prayer and discussion with Jeremy, she agreed to go with A.I.M. to Tanzania for eight months and flew out at the end of August. Even there, God had valuable preparation planned for her. Two of those months were spent in the bush and Rachel was able to observe how others coped in a primitive situation. In God's economy, nothing is wasted. He was preparing His children for the place He had already prepared for them.

Meanwhile, when Jeremy returned to the Bible College after Easter, he had sent a letter to Bill Leach, the General Secretary of the Qua Iboe Fellowship, expressing his interest in Burkina Faso. Bill was delighted to think that at last God might be about to answer the prayers for missionaries in Burkina Faso and suggested that Jeremy should attend the Qua Iboe London conference in September. At the conference, he spent as much time as possible talking to Bill, Jim Weir, the Scottish representative and Sid Garland, a missionary who was home on furlough. They answered his questions and discussed possibilities though they were aware that Jeremy knew more about the situation in Burkina Faso than they did! The one thing he couldn't tell them was whether he would be applying as a single or married man.

Having finished Bible College, Jeremy needed a job so he began working as the caretaker of his church, Emmanuel Church in Northwood, a church that would prove to be a great support to him in the years to come. Before Rachel left, they had planned that Jeremy should fly out to visit her at Christmas time. By this time he was sure enough of Rachel's feelings for him to bring out some bridal magazines and an engagement ring which had been made in London for him.

They spent Christmas with some missionary friends, then one evening set out for a romantic evening in a nearby game park. They drove around, swam in the pool and enjoyed a meal together. Then, as the moon shone from a tropical sky bright with stars, Jeremy asked Rachel if she would marry him. She happily agreed.

They decided to plan for a June wedding even though Rachel would not return to England until April and this would leave her with only six weeks to prepare for the big day. The bridal magazines were put to good use, the help of Rachel's Mum was enlisted and everything was ready in time. After the wedding they set up home in the house that went along with Jeremy's caretaking job.

Their sights were now firmly fixed on serving God in Burkina Faso with the Qua Iboe Fellowship and the next few months were taken up with the lengthy application process and language learning. They began 1995 by attending the W.E.C. candidates' course. This was followed by a language learners' course at the Wycliffe Centre and French study at Les Cedres, a Christian language school in Paris, though by that time Rachel had other things on her mind besides language – she was expecting their first child!

Katie's arrival in February 1996 changed the Nash couple into the Nash family and, while Rachel looked after the new baby, Jeremy continued with language study. They joined the Qua Iboe supporters for the annual conference in May as accepted candidates. There they shared their hopes and dreams for the future in much the same way as Stanley Benington had done all those years ago. They too were assured of the love and prayers of those who listened to them in the conference room at Castle Erin, a conference centre on the north coast of Ireland.

The joy of those gathered at the conference was somewhat tinged with sadness, however, because Bill Leach, who had been greatly used of God to bring about the return into Burkina, had been called home to be with the Lord earlier in the year. John Cardoo had taken over as General Secretary and would be the one to oversee the arrangements for these new candidates.

For some of the older supporters it was like a dream come true – to think that God was leading Qua Iboe back into Burkina Faso! They were excited at the prospect of the mission once again extending its borders into another country and seeking to evangelise another people group. Just as the supporters in the thirties had taken the Lobis to their hearts, so they would take the Dagaris.

"We'll pray for you," one after another assured Jeremy and Rachel, "and we'll look forward to hearing what God will do through you."

The last few months at home passed in a whirl of arrangements, packing and travelling to churches and prayer groups to share their vision.

"We could have driven to Burkina by now," Jeremy remarked one day, "- so far we have travelled nearly three thousand miles on deputation. It's only two thousand four hundred to Burkina!" It was quicker to fly, of course, and a few hours after leaving London on 26th July 1996, they landed in Ouagadougou, the capital city of Burkina Faso.

30

FIRST IMPRESSIONS

Crowded vehicles…
..litter strewn streets
warm welcomes…
…beautiful countryside
insect-invaded house…
…poverty…
demon-possessed people
one bound in chains…
…bustling, colourful markets
…refreshing rains…
pot-bellied, smiling kids…
        death…funerals….
bumpy roads
…tough meat…
poor quality vegetables
early mornings…
    …early nights…
    ….siestas….

crowds staring at Katie...
...excited kids running up
African nights...noise
...drumming...voices...
thunder storms
....dusty streets
lively singing at church
......non-communication
cold showers....brrrrrr!
dead snake...pheww!
Baguettes...
...5a.m. mosque call....

"Well, what do you think, Jeremy?" asked Rachel. "Will that give our prayer partners a feel for our new way of life?"

"Yes, I think so. Now, what else do we need to tell them? We need to say that we have arrived safely and that our freight actually arrived before we did! Quite a miracle, that was."

"We have settled in well here at Gaoua," Rachel added, "and have met the W.E.C. team – we can tell them about the fellowship day yesterday. We have seen Eileen's house at Batie, where we will live until our own house is built."

"Now that's something that needs a lot of prayer. I don't know very much about building a house, apart from what I'm learning in the books I brought out and we really need to find a good builder – someone who can be trusted. We also have to sink a well - I've never done that before either! At least we have a plot. I thought it was very good."

"Yes," agreed Rachel, "it was great to see it, even though we couldn't walk around it in case we had a close encounter with a snake in all that long grass. I also enjoyed meeting the people in the Legmoin church. I'm looking forward to getting to know them."

Jeremy gave a rueful smile. "We'll have to learn some Dagari before we do that! I was glad the service that day was in French as well as Dagari – at least I could understand some of it. I hope we find someone soon who will be able to help us with our language learning."

"I found it hard enough learning French –I'm not really looking forward to having to tackle Dagari as well! Oh, we mustn't forget to ask the folks at home to pray for Katie and these anti-malarial tablets. I don't know how we are going to get the Paludrine down today. I don't think the jam is going to work now she knows what's inside it!"

"Maybe we could crush it into chocolate spread." Jeremy suggested. "I hate to waste chocolate spread but maybe it would be worth it…."

"I wonder how long it will be before she can swallow them down with a drink? At least she has kept in good health and seems to have adjusted well to her new home."

"Yes, we have such a lot to be thankful for. Let's get this letter finished and sent home – it's good to be able to keep everyone at home up to date."

By the time the next "Nash News" was sent home in November, the family had moved to Batie and had seen God answer their prayers about a builder in a wonderful way. The missionaries all took turns to go to Bobo, the second largest town, to do shopping for the whole team every two months. Their turn on the rota would come round about once a year, but they were given the opportunity to accompany another missionary on her trip so that they could learn how to do it. While in Bobo, they discussed their plans for the house and their need for a reliable builder with some Wycliffe (SIL) missionaries. They recommended a man called Barthelemy Soma, who was currently building a house for them.

As their return home was delayed by a day because of heavy rain, Jeremy took the opportunity to write a letter to Barthelemy, explaining the situation to him, though he wasn't too sure just how to get the letter to him. The delay turned out to be God-ordained.

Next day, as Jeremy began to load the car in preparation for the trip home, he noticed a stranger standing nearby, watching him. As was customary, they exchanged greetings, then the stranger asked,

"Where are you going to?"

"We're from Gaoua." Jeremy replied. "Where are you from?"

"I live in Banfora."

"Oh….. wonder if you could help me. Do you by any chance know of Barthelemy Soma? He is a builder from Banfora and I have a letter for him."

Jeremy was amazed when the man replied, "I'm Barthelemy Soma."

"Wow!! Well maybe you can read the letter right now and see what you think. We'd like you to build a house for us."

That extra day in Bobo Dioulasso also solved another problem for Jeremy and Rachel. While Jeremy was at the phone company, calling the mission to let them know of the delay, he felt prompted to get in touch with the C.M.A. mission in Ouagadougou, about a car they had for sale.

"I'm a missionary down in Gaoua," he said, "and I'm interested in buying the car you've advertised. I'd like to see it, but I'm currently in Bobo and will be leaving for Gaoua in the morning."

Once again he was amazed by the reply.

"Well, actually, the car is being driven down to Bobo right now. I can give you the number of our base there and you might be able to see the car this evening."

Later that evening they realised that God had provided, not just a car, but a dream car – a Mitsubishi 4x4 double–cab pickup with air conditioning! There was, however, still one problem to be sorted out. The mission needed to know within a week whether or not they wanted to buy it.

"We can't just say that we'll take it without consulting our own mission at home and that could take a long time – the Council only meets once a month."

Jeremy phoned John Cardoo in Belfast and was delighted to discover that the next Council meeting was due to take place that Tuesday. God's timing, as always, was perfect and the deal was completed satisfactorily before the week was out.

The rain not only caused problems for travelling but also for one of the churches near Batie. The Bambassou church had been built in the traditional way in which many of the buildings in Stanley' Benington's time would have been built, using mud and thatch as building materials. Previous rainy seasons had taken their toll and the church collapsed. A larger church was needed anyway because God had been at work in the lives of many people.

They had arrived in time to go with Eileen and the others to witness the burning of Ouoro's idols. The rain poured down but they still managed to light a fire. It was a dramatic introduction to the work. About twenty of Ouoro's family became Christians at the same time and that was a tremendous encouragement to the group of believers who met in the village.

As they rejoiced to see God at work in the villages surrounding Batie, they looked forward with expectant hearts to the time when they would be able to move to Legmoin, the place chosen and prepared for them. What miracles would they see Him do? What lives would they see Him change?

31

DAGARI AND DANGER

"Now I really need to get this straight," said Rachel, "market day is "daadaar"....and the day before market is "daabenedaar" ....oh dear, I've forgotten how to say two days before market. What is it, Jeremy?"

"Daaduudaar......... and the day after market is "daadyibio", he replied.

"Right, I think I've got that....................now, what about the other days?"

"Oh, they don't have special names, they're all called "dayere".

"But that's so confusing," Rachel groaned. "How will I ever make arrangements with people if the some of the days of the week have the same name?"

"If you are confused now," Jeremy laughed, "it's going to be worse when you go to Legmoin. "Daadaar" is Wednesday here in Batie, but it's Sunday in Legmoin!"

Language learning is always a long, frustrating task, fraught with many pitfalls and mistakes. It was, however, the main focus of their stay in Batie so they started a couple of days after moving and built each day's programme around it. Leon arrived in the morning to look after Katie who had a wonderful time being pushed around in her pushchair. She was entertained royally by Leon and her brothers and sisters and even managed a little language learning of her own! Meanwhile, Mum and Dad spent two hours in the morning with Omar and a further hour in the afternoon with Barnaby in an attempt to get to grips with the vagaries of the Dagari language. All went well for the first month or so, though Barnaby didn't always turn up when he should. Then they lost Omar's help at the same time as Jeremy was ill with a long bout of malaria. That was a rather discouraging time but the Christmas break and a pre-Christmas visit from Rachel's brother, Paul, refreshed and enthused everyone and they were able to resume their studies in the new year. Barnaby agreed to help for two hours each morning and proved himself to be much more reliable and was also more forthcoming and interactive during the lessons – a real answer to prayer.

The months in Batie went by –Jeremy and Rachel learnt a new language and passed their first examination in it. They adapted to a new culture, the house at Legmoin took shape under the skilled hands of Bathelemy and Katie took her first steps. She was a happy, contented child, despite occasional bouts of sickness and a constant battle with heat rash which was eventually brought under control.

Their relationship with Barthelemy grew to such an extent that he invited them to attend his wedding at the end of June. They were looking forward to it and set out on the road to Banfora with great anticipation. They had a blow out along the way but managed to stop the car without any problem. Such things are a common occurrence on the bad roads, so they just changed the wheel and continued with their journey. The car was full with wedding guests, including Pastor Zougbile, and they all enjoyed the opportunity to chat together as they drove along.

Suddenly a young lad on a bicycle in front of them turned to watch an oncoming car and drifted into their path. When Jeremy blew his horn at him, the young lad turned so violently that he fell off his bike right in front of them. Jeremy swerved to miss him and to miss the oncoming vehicle, losing control of the car, which fish-tailed along the murram road and ended up ploughing up an embankment.

"Jesus save us! Jesus save us!" shouted Elischeba.

"God help us!" cried Adelaide.

"Jer…..em….y!" yelled Rachel, as the car swerved from side to side.
It eventually came to an abrupt halt in the soft earth, narrowly missing some trees. The luggage on the roof shot forward, broke off the aerial and bounced off the bonnet. They would later thank God that the accident had happened where it did as there were huge ditches along much of the rest of the road.

During all of this violent motion, sixteen-month-old Katie sat strapped in her car seat, calmly reading a book. When the car stopped, she looked up quizzically as if to say, "can you please drive more carefully, Dad, I keep losing my page."

Pastor Zougbile unfortunately had a gash on his head, so he and Jeremy had to leave the others at the wedding and go to Banfora Hospital to get it stitched. They missed the whole wedding.

The day's traumas weren't over yet – Rachel enjoyed the wedding but it was hot and she was thirsty and the water bottle had been left in the car with Jeremy at the hospital. She was shy and didn't want to make a fuss so she didn't ask for water, thinking that she would be able to manage. Unfortunately, she became very dehydrated and was quite sick that evening.

It hadn't been a very good day but without the protecting hand of God, it could have been so much worse. The car was undamaged and Pastor Zougbile's injury healed up very quickly.

32

LIFE IN LEGMOIN

"Jeremy, where's the kerosene for the lamps? The sun is starting to set."

"I'm sure it's in the store room here...." called Jeremy, "oh no, that's the petrol........... wait a minute.....it says petrole......that's the French for kerosene......confusing isn't it!"

"I just need some light, that's all," said Rachel wearily, "I haven't any food prepared. I've been so busy unpacking."

"I want some tea," piped up a little voice.

"Oh Katie, please stop whining, I'm doing my best. I know you're hungry."

"O.K. the lamp's full...." Jeremy was relieved that something was sorted out. "Now where have you put the matches? Didn't we bring the matches? I'm sure we had some when we left Batie. I can't see a thing..... where's the torch? The sun goes down so fast here! We'll have to start getting ready for the evening a little earlier tomorrow. It'll be great when we get our solar panel up."

"I want some tea........where's my teddy?"

Katie wasn't too impressed with how things were going on the Nash family's big day – 26th July 1997, exactly one year since they had landed at Ouagadougou airport. It was the day of the move to their new home at Legmoin – the place prepared for them. Katie, however, knew nothing of the significance of the date. All she knew was that she was hungry and Teddy was lost and something had to be done about it – now!

It wasn't long before the lamps were lit, the food prepared, the beds made and Teddy found. Everyone settled down for their first night in their new home, exhausted but happy to be in Legmoin at last.

The next few weeks were incredibly busy. Shelves had to be put up, curtains had to be hung, a bookcase had to be made and everything had to be unpacked. There was the added pressure of having to get used to living without electricity or running water and, to crown it all, Katie took a bout of bacterial dysentery so most of Rachel's time was spent looking after her.

Legmoin was a village about four kilometres off the road from Batie to Gaoua. It was a typical Dagari village – the red laterite road led into the market place, past the scattered homes and farms of the villagers and past the police station on the edge of the village. The little wood and grass trading booths were arranged untidily around a big tree and people greeted one another as they walked or cycled through the village on their way to their farms or the dispensary or the school. There was little paid work and most people lived on what they could produce on the farmland.

The farms were close to the houses and chickens and guinea fowl squawked around the feet of the mothers as they prepared the food in the courtyards outside the houses. Children ran in and out or helped on the farms or herded the cows or goats or sheep.

A red and white telephone antenna stood on a small hill on the outskirts of the village and from there a great expanse of green bush stretched to the far horizon – land largely untouched by civilisation, largely unchanged since the Creator God spoke the word and brought it into being.

Their house sat on the edge of the village, to one side of a two hectare plot that included the small building in which the believers met to worship God each Sunday.

The solar panel and the piping for the water pump were eventually purchased in September and made a big difference to their quality of life – having light in the evenings meant that studying could be done and letters could be written in greater comfort, while the luxury of having running water was just unbelievable. The little house at Legmoin was beginning to feel more and more like home.

In the months that followed, they were able to establish something of a routine, still with a big emphasis on language learning. By September, they were able to write in their prayer letter:

"Each morning Marceline arrives to draw water from the well and help in the house and then at 8:30 Alice comes to play with Katie and Rudolph comes to do a few hours language study with us. All three belong to the Legmoin church. Marceline and Alice only speak Dagari, which will be good for our Dagari!...............In the afternoons we often go to the market place to practise our Dagari. Katie is a great conversation starter, especially as she loves the local snack food which delights the ladies sitting cooking it. Please pray that we would make good contacts and relationships and for boldness to take every opportunity to share the good news of Jesus."

They continued to be encouraged as they saw God working among the churches in the area. While their house was being built, the Legmoin church had also put up a new simple mud building with a tin roof and the church began meeting there soon after they moved in. It was such a joy for them to deepen their friendship with Pastor Zougbile, his wife Elischeba and their two children, Tychique and Josias.

One area of concern for them in the Legmoin church was that no one seemed to have a burden to reach the children in a way that was relevant to them.

"You know, I think I'll try to start a Sunday School," said Jeremy one day.

"What a good idea," Rachel encouraged him, "the children would love that. But where would you hold it? The church has only one room at the moment."

"Well, it wouldn't really need to be inside - maybe we could just let the children sit under a tree or something......."

"Who would do the teaching?" was Rachel's next question. "Your Dagari isn't really good enough yet......."

"I've been thinking about that. You know those Bible stories that Rudolph recorded for us? I could write out the story, then read it back to the children and use the flannelgraph pictures to illustrate it. Maybe one of the young men from the church could help me until my Dagari gets better, by repeating the story in good Dagari."

Everyone approved of the idea and the preparations were made. The flannelgraph pictures were organised, Joel agreed to help with interpretation and soon eight children were meeting regularly for Sunday School. Their proficiency in the language increased, with the help of Alfred, a villager with a reasonable level of French and a grammar course for another language. As Jeremy gained confidence, he found that he could do the teaching himself without having to rely on Joel so much.

Jeremy was thrilled to see evidence of the hand of God as he travelled with Zougbile from village to village. His visits to Bambassou were particularly encouraging. The believers there were working hard to complete a church building and the Lord was pouring out His blessing. By the time they moved into Legmoin, there were forty adults and twenty children attending the services in Bambassou and a growing number were turning to Christ, marking their conversion by the dramatic public burning of their idols. It was a special cause for rejoicing when two elderly heads of family decided to follow Jesus. One of them was the chief of the "bor", the initiation ceremony. Knowing that, in thirty years of work with the sister people group, the Birifor, hardly any of the older folk had been converted, Jeremy and Rachel were aware that this was an incredible breakthrough. God had surely been preparing the people to receive His word.

In the period between the harvest and the beginning of the rainy season, the Dagari people had less work to do, so Jeremy took the opportunity at that time to introduce some of the believers to the picture book "Good News". This programme, produced by Gospel Recordings International, had been introduced to Jeremy and Rachel by an Australian couple, whom they had met in Paris. It consisted of a picture book and forty short Bible stories recorded on to a tape cassette in the Dagari language. He hoped that if he taught two believers from Karmateon and Bambassou how to use the tapes, they would be able to pass on what they had learnt to their fellow believers at a later date. Jeremy realised that many of the believers had little knowledge even of well known Bible stories and he saw this as a way to address the problem.

He and Pastor Zougbile also hoped to start evangelism in a new village, Ouadiel, in the new year. They had visited the village in June, met the villagers and the chief, who had given them an invitation to return and speak again. They were very encouraged by this and also by the fact that there were already two Christians living in the village. Jeremy was excited about all the plans that were being made, but, like Stanley Benington before him, he found that sometimes God sees fit to change the plans of his people.

33

KATIE'S CRISES

By September, Rachel was fairly sure that she was going to have another baby. She and Jeremy were delighted at the possibility and shared that excitement with their parents and with John Cardoo, the General Secretary of the Qua Iboe Fellowship. They knew that most other missionary mothers had their babies in Ferkessedougou, in the Ivory Coast, and decided that they would do the same. The hospital was better equipped than the one in Ouagadougou and some western missionary doctors worked there.

The W.E.C. team conference took place in November and while they were there, they sat their second language examination. Eileen and two Dagari Christians from Legmoin were the examiners and they all gathered in Eileen's office. The fifteen minute examination was made more difficult than usual because both Jeremy and Rachel had had a bout of malaria and the treatment for it produces deafness and tinnitus – not the best circumstances in which to do an oral examination in a tonal language! Despite the problems, they both managed to pass – probably thanks to lenient examiners, they thought.

An earlier summons to the office had left them feeling rather apprehensive – had they done something wrong? Again?

"What is it?" they asked.

"John Cardoo has been in touch with us. The mission council thinks that you should go home early to have your baby."

It was difficult to know how to react – should they express regret at having to return early to the U.K..... at having to leave the work they had started? Certainly they would be sorry to leave Legmoin and all their friends there but it was difficult to contain the joy they felt at the prospect of seeing their families again and having their new baby in familiar surroundings. Somehow they managed to keep straight faces and to make the appropriate response until they left the office. Their smiles broke out as soon as the door was closed!

Christmas was very special that year – it was the first one in their new home, Katie was old enough to be excited about it and Rachel's parents arrived on 7th December for a five week visit and so were able to join in the fun. Rachel decorated the home for Christmas and they brought in a branch from one of the trees outside, put it in a pot and hung decorations from it. Presents were put around the "Christmas tree" just like at home. Rachel's Mum brought out a nativity scene from England and Rachel had a shirt made for her dad from the traditional Christmas cloth produced by the E.P.E. Church.

Their celebration of Christmas with the Legmoin church was rather different to a British celebration. The Christmas Eve service lasted all night and Rachel's Mum commented that the lamp-lit church with its low roof and mud walls probably looked quite like the original stable. The Christians, almost all of whom were dressed in the Christmas cloth, spent the night singing, then praying, then listening to a sermon, then repeating the process all over again. They had a break half way through for a Christmas treat of coffee, kindly supplied by Rachel.

A Christmas dinner of rice and goat stew, was eaten all together in the church. They enjoyed it very much, though Rachel's Dad didn't enjoy the aftermath – he was violently sick later on in the day! The new Sunday School took part in the service and Jeremy did a flannelgraph presentation to demonstrate how the children were taught each week.

Katie enjoyed having her grandparents to stay and had practised how to say "Granny" and "Grandpa" before they arrived. They both enjoyed the visit, though Rachel's Mum was quite ill at the beginning and discovered rather more about the local medical facilities than she would have wished. By the end of the visit, Katie had learnt a new word association – "Granny / toilet"!

After Christmas they all set off for a family holiday in Ivory Coast. They spent some time in San Pedro, a coastal resort and then changed location to the mountain town of Man. It was a much-needed time of rest and relaxation, swimming and walking and visiting friends.

On the way back through Bobo to leave Granny and Grandpa at the airport, they stopped at a hotel for lunch. Katie enjoyed some ice-cream, then Jeremy and Granny took Katie swimming in the hotel pool, while Rachel and her Dad climbed up some steps to take a photograph.

Suddenly, Rachel heard Katie screaming at the top of her voice and she rushed down the steps to see what had happened. Blood was pouring out of Katie's mouth.

"She slipped on the swimming pool steps and banged her face on the edge," Jeremy explained.

Rachel examined her mouth and found that two of Katie's front teeth were missing.

"Maybe if we find them, they could be put back again," Rachel suggested, so they searched for the little teeth, and then made their way to get medical help. The nurse cleaned up Katie's face but told them there was no point trying to replace baby teeth as they would fall out eventually anyway. Everyone was very upset by the experience and poor Katie had a swollen, sore face for quite a few days.

They said their goodbyes to Rachel's parents, knowing of course that they would see them again in a few short weeks. They stayed on in the capital to do shopping and other business. Katie was running a temperature so they visited a French doctor who gave them a prescription for medicine. On their way to get the medicine, they called at a restaurant for something to eat. Rachel started to give a bottle to Katie who suddenly threw her head back and began to convulse.

An Austrian lady who was sitting nearby saw what was happening and shouted for someone to bring ice.

"Come with me!" she urged.

Rachel bundled Katie up in her arms and ran to the car. Her rescuer put her foot on the accelerator and her hand on the horn and headed back to the French doctor. All Rachel and Jeremy could do was pray,

"Keep breathing! Keep breathing!" she whispered to Katie. Once in the medical centre, the doctor gave her valium and the crisis passed. Afterwards they marvelled at the wonderful way God had provided help just when they needed it.

The next five weeks flew past in a flurry of packing up the house and making arrangements to leave. They continued to do language study but it was hard to concentrate on it in the midst of all the excitement. Everything in the house was packed into barrels and put in a secure storeroom. The services of a night guard were secured and the blue Mitsubishi drove slowly out to the road to Gaoua …….the road to home!

34

TEARS AND TESTIMONIES

Timothy Edward Nash made his entrance into the world on 22nd April that year. The furlough months seemed to fly past. Jeremy took a three-week course to improve his French at the London Alliance Francaise and they continued to work on the Dagari language, using some tapes of Bible stories and their language notes. They took part in various Q.I.F. conferences and prayer meetings and enjoyed the opportunity to share what God had been doing in their lives and among the Dagari people. They learned that a new Wycliffe Bible Translator was to be sent to Djiebougou, about 80 miles away from Legmoin and they looked forward to making contact with him from time to time, to help each other with language study, though they reckoned that they would benefit most from the arrangement, as Colin was a gifted linguist.

They left England on 14th September and soon settled back into the routine of life in Legmoin. Language study with their neighbour, Simeon, took place each morning while Alice looked after Katie and Timothy. Then in the afternoons, Rachel spent time with the children, reading books, painting and playing or in the garden, where she had planted trees and flowers.

Snakes were an ever-present danger, though they were particularly prevalent in October and November, when the grass was high. Angelina, who helped them in the home, got bitten as she took food to someone's house. She recovered from the bite but there were many who didn't. Two children from Zinka died that season.

Early one morning Rachel heard a shout and saw Angelina on the path outside their house. She had a large rock in her hand and was looking threateningly at the ground.

"I think there's a snake, Jeremy," she said. "Get the rake and go and help her!"

Rachel and Katie followed Jeremy outside but Angelina had killed the snake before they got there. When they were sure it was really dead, they brought Katie over.

"Look, Katie, that's a snake. What do we do if we see a snake?"

Katie knew the answer to that question – they had practised their snake drill often enough!

"Run", she said confidently, "and shout 'snake! snake! snake!'"

"At least now she knows what a snake looks like," Rachel said to Jeremy, as they made their way back to the house.

"I do hope we get the snake zapper soon," Jeremy remarked. "I must admit I'll feel happier when we have both the serum and the zapper."

The zapper was a new treatment which produced an electric shock that in some way neutralized the venom of snakes and scorpions. The area around the bite was zapped a number of times and the pain eased about twenty minutes later. They knew that they could save many lives with it, as no serum was available locally and what was available in Ouagadougou was too expensive. By the time they wrote their next prayer letter in April, the zapper had been purchased and put to good use. In two and a half months, they had used it eight times. It wasn't always effective because often the people would try the local medicines and treatments first or would be afraid of the strange, painful sensation of the powerful shock that was administered.

Jeremy disciplined himself to go visiting in the afternoons and decided to cycle on his own to the next village, Zinka, which was about three kilometres from home. The people in Zinka didn't know him so well, so it was very profitable just to visit in their courtyards and talk with them as they did their daily chores. Their reaction to the realisation that he could understand and even speak a little Dagari always amused him.

Until that time, Pastor Zougbile and his family had been living in rented accommodation. When they were forced to move house for the third time, he and Jeremy decided that the time had come to build a house for Zougbile. They travelled to Gaoua to see Pastor Pierre, the Church president. Zougbile explained the situation.

"We really need a pastor's house," he said.

The President, who didn't understand that they were talking about building a house, gave a little shrug of his shoulders.

"Well, what's that to do with me? You can find a house yourself and pay the rent," he replied.

When they explained further, he merely said,

"Well that's up to you."

Zoubile and Jeremy assumed that he was giving his permission and went back to Legmoin to make the necessary arrangements.

They copied the design of other Pastors' houses in the area, except that Zougbile decided that he would like to have an indoor shower.

By December, a road had been cleared so that a lorry could bring loads of sand and 3000 bricks had been ordered. They would be cut from a laterite pit not far from Jeremy and Rachel's house Normally when a pastor's house was built, the church people would join together to do the work and the church committee decreed that Zougbile's house should be built that way too.

The problems arose when Jeremy and Zougbile began to work out who in the church would be available to do the building. Since half the members were women and some of the men were not able to help, there were only two men who were suitable. They felt that it wasn't fair on them having to do all the work, so they said they would pay them for their work. Everyone seemed happy with the plan and the work began.

All new missionaries who work in association with the E.P.E. church (Eglise Protestante Evangelique) undergo an evaluation at the end of their probationary period before they are accepted as permanent missionaries. Jeremy and Rachel weren't particularly worried about the evaluation, as things seemed to be going quite well. Two members of the local church were sent to the Committee Locale where their work was discussed. A few weeks later, the results of their evaluation were given to them at a meeting with the Church President and some of the W.E.C. leaders.

It was a difficult two hours. Very little was said to encourage them. Most of the comments made were critical. They had obviously not obtained the correct permission for the building of the pastor's house............ they shouldn't have paid the men for working on the house....... on and on it went. They emerged from the meeting feeling battered and shell-shocked, with their probationary period extended by another six months.

Back at Legmoin, of course, life went on as usual and the next morning found Jeremy shovelling sand into the back of a truck so that it could be dumped. It was hard, back-breaking work and the hot sun drained his energy. Rachel came out to speak to him and something just broke inside them. They stood together at the back of the truck and cried and cried. It felt as though all the work they had done and all the sacrifices they had made counted for nothing.

Even in the midst of the heartache, however, God was working in the lives of the people. Zougbile met with Jeremy in the old church one day and they planned their strategy for evangelism. They decided to target three villages, Piri, Opore and Ouelba. The chief in each village was consulted and permission to preach was obtained.

One Sunday morning during the service at Legmoin, they announced their intention to visit Ouelba and suddenly realised that Ouelba was one of their "prepared places". A new Christian had joined them that very Sunday and when he stood up to introduce himself, he told them that he had come from Ouelba. He had come to know the Lord while working in Ivory Coast and had only just returned to his village.

"He's the first fruit of the harvest to come," thought Jeremy.

On their first visit, Amos, one of the Karmateon Christians, gave a powerful testimony to the grace of God in his life. Many of those who listened knew him and recognised that he was speaking the truth because they had seen how God had worked in his life, delivering him from idol worship and addiction to drink. They had also seen his wholehearted commitment to God when his faith remained firm, even in the face of the loss of his seven-year-old son as a result of a snake bite, The way Amos put it was that he had "taken hold of God with both hands".

The "Nash News" told the story of what happened next:

"Four days later we returned and began by singing which attracted a good number of people. At the end of the meeting we said we would pray for the village, but if anyone wanted to join us and follow Jesus, they would be welcome. An old man first came and then one by one, four others joined him. They each told us why they were ready to follow Jesus. Another very old man said he wanted to die but now he could do so in peace."

They watched the burning of their idols, a scene very similar to many witnessed by Stanley Benington. It was a most exciting and encouraging experience.

The purchase of a new motorbike enabled Jeremy to travel even further afield and he began to visit the other Dagari Churches to encourage the believers. He and Zougbile began a Thursday meeting in Ouadiel, which was attended by the new believers from Ouelba. They met to teach and sing with the Christians and the small group soon grew to twelve adults and about thirty children.

God had really been blessing the work in Bambassou. Even some of the old folk had turned from their idols and numbers had increased greatly. A new church had been built and a new pastor was sent to serve the Lord in that area. Unfortunately, he was from the Birifor people group and didn't understand all the local customs. He brought quite a few possessions with him and the Dagari people don't like it if someone has more than them. They became jealous and began stealing or killing his animals. Someone then tried to poison his land and at that stage, he went to the police, as he would have done in his own village. The thief was caught and put in prison but the people were angry.

"That is not the thing to do," they said. It looked to them as though this new pastor had come just to put people into prison! He explained why he had done what he did and asked their forgiveness.

"If that is not what is done in a Dagari village, I will do it your way," he promised.

He had no more trouble and the Lord continued to bless the work there.

The Church at Legmoin was also a source of encouragement. Although there were no new believers from the village itself, new converts from other villages were joining them almost every week and the little group had grown to over forty. In many cases they were drawn to the Lord through difficult circumstances or illness and came to the church to ask for prayer.

Nangmin-bon was a teenager who had a badly infected elbow. At his request, Zougbile and Jeremy went to his house to pray for him. They were shocked at the state of his elbow – the infection had eaten right into the bone and had resulted in such terrible pain that he had not slept for many weeks. The two men prayed for him and were greatly encouraged when they visited him the next day, to find that the pain had gone and that he had slept well. They kept praying for complete healing and the pain stayed away. He also began attending church and so they prayed that he would put his trust in Jesus, not just for healing but also for salvation.

No matter how much they prayed, however, the elbow never healed up completely and Jeremy couldn't understand why God had only gone half way to answer their prayers. Eventually, they took him to Bobo to see if the doctors there could cut out the infection. They couldn't do anything for him so when Jeremy saw the German doctor in Gaoua, he asked her if it would be possible to amputate the lower arm. She was horrified at the suggestion.

"No, no, we can't do that!" she said. "Just keep washing it well and it will clear up."

They went back to Legmoin and did as she suggested but it got no better. Then he developed a cough and had to go to the Gaoua hospital for treatment. There they discovered that he had TB and put him on treatment for that. To their surprise, the infected elbow responded too and he was healed. He continued to attend the church, enjoyed listening to the Dagari tapes and did put his trust in Jesus. He lost mobility in his arm but was able to work and even went to Ivory Coast to work for several months, coming back the proud owner of a bicycle.

They prayed with many people but of course they didn't all have the happy ending of Nangmin-Bon's story. On one of their visits to Ouelba, they were asked to pray with a six year old boy who had a badly infected eye. They arrived at night and examined the eye by torchlight. It was a horrible sight – the eye was swollen bigger than an egg. He was not in any pain and they prayed that the swelling would go down. As time went on, they discovered that the growth was cancerous and sadly, he died soon afterwards.

PRW
26/9/02

35

A WET SEAT AND A HARD FLOOR

Their annual holiday that year was spent with Jeremy's Dad. Unfortunately he hurt his back on his first day in Burkina and spent most of his visit to Legmoin flat on his back. It wasn't until the day before they left for Ivory Coast that he was able to explore the village. They all enjoyed the holiday in San Pedro and Man in July and also spent some time buying children's books for the lending library they had begun. They thought this would be a good way to begin to build relationships with the children in Legmoin and would also help these children with their studies, as teaching in the schools was done in French.

A large blue trunk was divided into sections, tickets were placed inside each book and the lending library was ready. The local children soon got the idea and benefited greatly from having access to a wide range of books. They hoped that the relationships that would grow from it might eventually lead to the beginning of a youth work in association with the church.

September was a difficult month. It was decided that Jeremy would collect a returning WEC couple, the Swaffields, from the Ouagadougou airport, so he set out on the day of their expected arrival very early in the morning. He didn't realise until he got to Gaoua that there had been very heavy rain, but he checked with the police at Djiebougou and they assured him that the road had not been closed. He and his passenger travelled on.

The road was muddy and slippery so he put the motor into four-wheel drive and slowly made his way through the puddles. When they came to a rain barrier, they were allowed to go on because it was really intended to stop heavy lorries from churning up the road in wet weather.

Suddenly they came to a section of the road that was completely submerged in water, Some local men were helping to carry motorbikes across the flood and they shouted up to Jeremy,

"Wait there and we'll come and help you too!"

As they went across, Jeremy could see that the water was up to their waists at the deepest part and his heart sank. He waited for about ten minutes and they still hadn't returned to help him so he said to his companion,

"Look, we'll just get in and have a go. It will be alright if we just keep going."

Famous last words!

Jeremy put the car into second gear and inched forward into the water. It got deeper and deeper and eventually came right up to the bonnet of the car. Suddenly the engine gave a groan of protest and stopped in the middle of the flood. Water started to pour into the cab, soaking his shoes, then his trousers, then the seat he was sitting on.

"Oh no! what ever do we do now?" wondered Jeremy.

The men who had offered to help came and pushed the motor over to the far side of the flood. Jeremy let it sit for some time before he tried to start it but it was no good - the engine was dead. He sent for a mechanic and tried to fiddle with the engine himself. Two hours later he tried again and this time the motor started – accompanied by clouds of smoke! It was really jerky but it was moving so he decided to try to reach the next town.

Along the way he stopped to phone Rachel who was then able to arrange for someone else to meet the Swaffields. Saying a prayer of thanks for the fairly good communications in Burkina, he continued on his way. He met the mechanic coming along the road and he took Jeremy back to his workshop, where he changed the oil and tried to dry out the engine. Jeremy finally reached Ouagadougou at ten o'clock that night, exhausted but glad to be there, even though the car was still trailing a cloud of smoke.

When the mechanic in the city examined the engine, he found that two of the pistons had been damaged and the whole engine had to be taken out so that they could be fixed. The short drive through the water had cost a lot of money and a ten-day wait in Ouagadougou.

When he finally did return home, he found that Rachel had been suffering too – both children had been sick and she herself had succumbed to an attack of 'flu'. A miserable time had been had by all. Such are the joys of missionary work!

A visit from Rachel's parents in October cheered them up. This time it was a working visit as Pauline was able to teach English at the new college in Legmoin and Neil became the odd-job man.

While they were there, Jeremy took the opportunity to make a five-day visit to Wadiel, a small village about eleven kilometres away. It would be a good language learning experience, as Jean-Paul and Marthe, the couple with whom he stayed, spoke no English and hardly any French. He packed his drinking water, a mosquito net, a torch, some clothes, toilet paper and a wash kit in a backpack, tied on his purple and yellow sleeping mat behind the saddle of his bicycle and set off through the village, feeling rather like an intrepid pioneer missionary – a real "Stanley Benington moment"!

Jean-Paul, Marthe and their three children made him very welcome. They had set aside one of their rooms for his use and had placed a chair in it. Jeremy hung his mosquito net from the roof beams and settled in to village life. One of the first requirements was to greet the village chief and the government delegate, who welcomed him to their village.

It was an interesting experience – an opportunity to identify more fully with the people he had come to serve. Marthe took pains to feed him well. He and Jean-Paul ate separately from the rest of the family, as is the custom, and Jeremy learned to place his spoon a certain way on the plate to indicate that he was finished. Water would then be brought so that he could wash his hands.

There was, of course, no bathroom in the house. The bath was simply a bucket behind a mud wall and the toilet was a suitable bush! He got used to those facilities but the sleeping arrangements were another matter. It was impossible to get comfortable on the sleeping mat on the hard floor and he slept little. He rose with the dawn each morning, aching in every bone. He even tried sitting in the chair to sleep but that was no better.

He accompanied Jean-Paul wherever he went and helped him on his farm, using a "daba", a rather primitive wood and metal tool, to weed between the tall rows of millet. They came across a mouse hole one day and when the mouse dashed out, Jeremy was astonished to see the men chase after it, excited at the possibility of some extra food.

The local river was very high, so it was a good time to go fishing. The men would throw little bits of food into the water, then actually catch the fish using pieces of string with soap on the end. The fish they caught were enjoyed in the evening, cooked in the soup and eaten with "tow", the local staple food.

The evenings were spent sitting in the courtyard round a lamp, listening to stories, sometimes the traditional stories of the Dagari people and sometimes funny stories that they all enjoyed. Often songs were interwoven into the stories.

As he rode back home along the dusty path, he thought that his experience had been an invaluable one. He knew for sure that he would have a more compassionate heart for the suffering of the people, especially each time he remembered his restless nights on the hard floor. He understood now why the Dagari greetings often included the questions,

"You're up?" and "Are you strong?"

By November they had completed the second phase of their building programme – a schoolroom for Katie and an office for Jeremy. It was good to be able to actually "go" to school and to the office. They were also making plans for a new worker. They had met Casimir Bouagnan while on furlough and had been impressed by his enthusiasm for the work in Burkina. He had arrived in Gaoua in September and had completed two months orientation with the W.E.C. team there.

Before he went to Legmoin, Jeremy and Rachel searched for suitable accommodation for him and found a house in the village. When Casimir came out to see it, however, he had a problem with the arrangement,
"I can't live in the village – the people might attack me," he said. He went on to explain that because he came from Ivory Coast and there was fighting between the Burkinabe migrant workers and the Ivorians, he was afraid for his life. Jeremy tried to reassure him by saying that the people all knew him and Pastor Zougbile and really if anyone attacked Casimir, it would be like attacking them. He wasn't convinced, however, and when he talked to Eileen at Gaoua, it was apparent that he really wanted to live with the Nashes. So it was arranged that he would occupy the new schoolroom and at the end of November, he moved in.

Right from the start, it was obvious that he was unsettled. He found it hard to sleep and the level of poverty in which the people lived was a real culture shock to him. He had been sure that he would learn the language quickly but with all the unsettled emotions he had, he didn't make much progress.

He had to return to London, where he had been studying before going to Burkina, to collect some of his belongings. After spending a month there, he returned to Legmoin but stayed only a short time. At the May mission conference, without giving anyone prior notice, he simply announced that he was going home. No amount of discussion could persuade him otherwise and he left the following week. It was a disappointment to Jeremy and Rachel and also the Qua Iboe Fellowship, who had sent him out amid great rejoicing at the acceptance of the first African missionary.

36

VISITS AND VISITORS

Rachel opened the note which had been sent through to her from Jeremy and smiled,

"I'm sitting under a tree at Victorian's house," she read. "Etienne is helping him make a door. I've a new perspective on poverty – trying to remove old nails with a clawless hammer and an old bit of metal. Absolutely no useful tools!"

Jeremy was away again for five days, this time to stay with Jacques and his family at Baupiel, about seven miles from Legmoin. On this occasion he saw a completely different aspect of village life, because Jacques was a trader. They visited various markets, where Jacques would set up his stall and Jeremy would spend his time talking to the people, practising his Dagari. The largest one was the Wednesday market in Batie. The two of them rode the twenty miles on bicycles and Jeremy enjoyed the camaraderie of the journey. Everyone shouted a greeting as they passed and some even stopped for a chat along the roadside. He was tired and dusty at the end of it but the experience was worth it.

When he gazed around one of the smaller markets and realised that there had probably never been a Christian witness in that village, he was impressed once again with the tremendous need in that area – so many villages still had not been reached with the Gospel. He and men like Zougbile had been called to a huge task, one which would require the grace and power of God Himself to complete.

Living with the people and watching the struggle of their daily lives, seeing them try to mend things with stones and useless tools reminded him once again of the tension in which he and Rachel lived – the tension of being in two worlds at once. They lived in a comfortable home, had the use of a car and were rich by Burkinabe standards, yet a short distance away, in the village, there was real poverty and every day brought people with genuine needs to their door.

So it was perhaps inevitable that, although their designated ministry was 'evangelism and church-planting', they became involved in humanitarian aid. Their poor fund started just with them helping a few people themselves but when Jeremy's family heard about it, they offered to help and sent some money for that purpose. When folks came to their door with prescriptions they couldn't afford, or needing financial help to have an operation in the hospital at Gaoua or even further afield in Bobo, they had the joy of being able to give assistance and the satisfaction of seeing those people cured of their illness. Two men from Bambassou were able to have hernia operations that they could not otherwise have afforded. It was a good way of following the example of Jesus and living as He lived.

The words 'joy' and 'satisfaction' could not always be used to describe how they felt! There were many frustrations and difficulties, not least of which was the suspicion that sometimes the people were only interested in coming to the mission house or to the church for the practical help they were given. Jeremy particularly struggled with this and often felt tense and annoyed when those he helped seemed to abuse his trust. Eventually, he came to realise that he was really battling with the whole process of 'dying to self' and determined to try to accept the things he couldn't change and trust God in all aspects of life. It wasn't easy but Rachel remarked that "the house was a much calmer place" as a result!

The New Year (and new millennium) began with a visit from two Belfast Bible College students. Andrew and Serena de Gruchy and their baby, Naomi, spent three weeks of their student elective with Jeremy and Rachel. They were able to join them for the burning of Pierre's idols in the village of Doudou.

Pierre had been very involved in the occult. His house was full of idols and fetishes and he was a medium who heard spirit voices. At one time the idols had told him to stop cultivating his farm and he had obeyed, despite knowing that he would be reduced to begging from others if he didn't grow his own food.

So when the spirit voices told him to destroy all his idols but to keep the rock which is above all other things, he went to Silas, a local Christian, who brought him to Zougbile and Jeremy. They counselled him and Zougbile realised that in fact the man was possessed by evil spirits. They advised him to burn all his idols and went to his house to witness the burning.

As the visitors looked on with great interest, Zougbile and Jeremy had the joy of helping him to bring out all his idols from their hiding places in his house, and watching while he set fire to them. The Christians gathered round in a gesture of support and many in the village looked on as he took this public step of commitment to Jesus.

Andrew was a carpenter and was able to make six new benches for the church. The Christians at Wadiel were still in the process of building their new church and joined the Legmoin services each Sunday, so the benches were greatly appreciated.

While Jeremy was busy with the church work, Rachel continued to home-school Katie and Timmy joined in too. It was a fulfilling task but also a rather frustrating one. There were days when great progress was made and there were aspects of the work that both children enjoyed very much but equally there were days when Katie was tired and difficult and either found everything 'boring' or wanted to choose what to do rather than take orders. When Jeremy was away there were also many interruptions to be dealt with and often work had to be set aside to help someone who came to the door with a problem.

One of the trips Jeremy made was to Bapla, where Colin Mills lived. They had first met Colin at the Wycliffe Bible Translators' centre in England, where they all did some language training and were thrilled to find that he would be working on the Dagari literacy and translation programme. He had visited them in April and they had agreed that Jeremy would spend a week with Colin in May. It was of mutual benefit – Jeremy was helped with his own language study and enjoyed watching the team at work on some tonal aspects of Dagari, while Colin enjoyed having someone from 'home' to talk to. His was a lonely existence, living on his own at the edge of a village, having few callers, working to a tightly structured schedule with only two other people. He hoped eventually to begin the translation of the New Testament into Dagari, which would be a tremendous asset to Jeremy and those involved in church-planting.

They decided to spend their annual holiday this time in England – a popular choice with Katie, who, in the weeks leading up to it, talked constantly about the aeroplane ride and the fact that "we'll have ice-cream every day!" On a more practical note Jeremy and Rachel hoped that the month in England would help to clear up Timmy's heat rash and that they would all return refreshed and ready to face the rigours of the last few months in Legmoin before returning home for a furlough. Little did they realise that those months would prove to be some of the most difficult they had experienced yet. What a blessing it is that God throws a veil over the future.

37

ORDEALS

"Rachel, do I put the eggs in altogether or one at a time?" called Jeremy from the kitchen.

Rachel smiled to herself – this was a bit like baking a cake by remote control.

"What a way to spend a birthday!" she thought.

She and Jeremy had been thrilled to discover that a new baby was on the way but, a few days earlier, she had realised that things were not going according to plan and had phoned Eileen for advice. She had taken that advice, which was why she was spending her birthday in bed, giving instructions to Jeremy who was making her birthday cake with Katie and Timmy's help.

When bedrest didn't improve the situation, she phoned the French Medical Centre in Ouagadougou.

"You need to come in right away!" they said.

"Oh I can't do that," she replied, "it's four hundred kilometres away! There's a local hospital at Gaoua."

"Well you should go there then," they advised.

That evening they drove the twenty-five miles to Gaoua, where the nurses checked Rachel and did a scan. When Rachel saw the screen, she knew that the baby had died. No heartbeat pulsed, nothing moved, no shape could be seen.

They returned to Legmoin, to let nature take its course and tried to explain to Katie and Timmy what was happening and why Mummy was lying on the settee.

"Sometimes babies come too early," they said, "and then they go to be with Jesus."

The children accepted this explanation without too much question.

By Sunday afternoon Rachel had started bleeding quite badly. She sent for the village midwife who advised her to go to hospital again, so they packed up clothes and things for the children and set off once more for Gaoua.

Eileen had been concerned about Rachel and had set out for Legmoin that same day. They met her on the road and she accompanied them to the hospital. Jeremy left her with Eileen and then brought the children to stay with the Swaffields. Julie's husband, Paul, was sick with malaria and was having hallucinations as a result of the treatment he was on but even so, Julie managed to cope with a rather tearful Katie and Timmy – it was the first time they had ever been away from both parents at the same time.

The nurses examined Rachel and decided that they would have to do a D & C. From what they said Rachel realised that they were going to carry out this procedure manually and without any anaesthetic!

"Can we have it done in theatre under anaesthetic?" they asked.

The nurses replied that it would be very expensive and seemed reluctant to bring in an anaesthetist or a gynaecologist.

"We will pay for it," Rachel pleaded but they could not be persuaded.

So she very bravely allowed them to begin the procedure, after Jeremy had gone to the hospital pharmacy and bought all the equipment they would need. It was the most excruciatingly painful thing she had ever experienced. She held on tightly to Eileen's hand and tried not to shout out but after some time, she had to tell them to stop.

"I can't take anymore," she said.

They stopped and left and Rachel breathed a sigh of relief – at least it was all over! Eileen had brought sheets and food and they got Rachel bedded down for the night. Jeremy stayed with her but neither of them got much sleep. Rachel was sore and the bed was too narrow for the two of them.

Next morning the nurses arrived - to finish the procedure! Half an hour later, it really was all over and Rachel went to Eileen's house to recover from her ordeal. Eileen and their other friends at the W.E.C. mission station looked after them until Rachel felt stronger.

Meanwhile Jeremy had his own ordeal to face. He returned to Legmoin to check the house and the fridge and to fetch some more clothes for the family. Everything seemed fine and he didn't go back to the house until a week later. He needed to collect some more things for their trip to the airport at Ouagadougou to meet John Cardoo and Jeremy Forsythe, from the Qua Iboe Fellowship.

When he opened the door he noticed a most awful, overpowering smell. He traced its cause to the fridge – during the week it had gone out and everything in the fridge and the freezer had begun to rot. A foul-smelling mixture of blood and water had dripped down through the fridge as the meat had defrosted. They had just filled it with foodstuff from the Bobo shopping trip so it was full to the brim. What a terrible job! He and one of the girls who helped them in the house had to throw almost everything out and clean the fridge and freezer really thoroughly to get rid of the smell. Even the precious Mars bars had to go! It seemed like the final straw, though he was very grateful that he had discovered it before they brought their visitors to the house!

They were encouraged by the visit from John and Jeremy. They visited several of the new churches and brought greetings to the Christians from Northern Ireland. They even braved the perils of riding pillion on motorbikes to visit some of the more remote villages. Jeremy showed them the new buildings at Wadiel and Karmateon and shared with them his joy at the recent conversion of Marthe, the wife of Jean-Paul, one of the leaders of the Wadiel church. This would mean that Jean-Paul could now apply to go to the EPE Lobiri Bible School. It would not have been possible for him to do so while Marthe was an unbeliever.

He also shared with them his aspirations for the little group at Tobo. At one time there had been quite a large thriving church in Tobo but sin had crept in and by the time they arrived attendance had dwindled to about ten people, who met under a tree. Jeremy began going to the church about once a month and took it on as one of his main responsibilities. As his grasp of the language got better, he began to preach in Dagari and it was good practice for him.

As time passed, he realised that something was wrong – the church wasn't growing, God wasn't blessing there the way he was in other places. On two occasions, they had tried to build a church but neither attempt had been successful. Jeremy had been reminded of the scriptural principle that unless the Lord builds the house, the labour is in vain. Then one of the Christians brought a non-Christian woman to live with him and they also knew that there had been other instances of immorality in the past.

Jeremy and Zougbile came to the conclusion that they should meet with the church for a day of repentance. They went over to Tobo one Sunday and after the service, met with the people to talk about how the sin of one person could affect others and about the need for repentance and forgiveness.

They confronted the man who was living with the non-Christian girl but he wasn't prepared to change his ways so they suggested that he would have to leave the church. Others used the day as an opportunity to put things right and to repent of past sin and at the end of the day, Jeremy encouraged them by saying that he knew that God would bless them for what they had done.

He sensed, however, that the growth would not come quickly but that it would last.

"Look at the maize," he said to them, "it grows up in a few months but does it last? No it dies quickly. But look at this tree – does it come up quickly? No, it takes many years but it lasts for a long time. I think that is how it is going to be."

As time passed by, Jeremy's prophetic words proved to be true. The first sign of God's favour was when the Christians completed a church building without any trouble. A further indication of His blessing was when Sammy, one of the group of believers at Tobo, was successful in a literacy training programme, which would qualify him to teach Dagari reading and writing courses in the churches. This would mean that when Colin and his team completed the Dagari New Testament, there would be people in the churches who could read it.

Satan continued to attack the little family in their final few months before furlough. Jeremy was plagued by bouts of malaria, which left him feeling washed out and also hindered him in the work he wanted to do. Despite this, he did manage to pass his final language examination in November.

Soon it was time to pack the barrels once again. In the midst of all the busyness, Timmy got sick. They didn't think too much of it to begin with, thinking it was just a virus. He had had a bout of malaria about five weeks earlier while they had been staying at Gaoua and they had found it almost impossible to get him to take his medicine. They had managed to encourage him to take about half the treatment but had then been forced to abandon the idea.

When he continued to be miserable and his temperature continued to be high, they brought him to Gaoua hospital, where they did a blood test to check for malaria. The nurses were very concerned at the test results.

"Is this blood test for him?" they enquired. "He's not leaving the hospital!"

The nurses announced their intention of putting in a line for a quinine drip. Jeremy tried to hold the little boy still, praying all the time,

"Please God, get it in first time!"

His prayers were answered and the nurses left them to watch Timmy and the drip. They knew little about attending a drip but were able to recognise the potential dangers of it running out or getting air in the line. They hadn't brought sheets so just laid Timmy on towels.

They stayed there all day and as Timmy began to feel better, they had an added problem to attend to – a lively two-year-old who wanted to jump on the bed and look out the window, still attached to his drip!

Next day the nurses took the drip out and Rachel washed down his bed (a hospital requirement). They stayed at the Gaoua mission station that night and became increasingly concerned as Timmy's temperature crept up again – 39 degrees.... 40 degrees.....41 degrees....

At that point, they went back to the hospital but were told just to keep on with the treatment they had been given and he would get better.

When they returned to Eileen's house, she had brought out her Christmas tree in an attempt to distract the children and Katie and Timmy spent a few happy hours helping her to decorate it.

A few days later, they were on their way to England. Poor Timmy was sick all the way home in the plane but eventually recovered without any more treatment. One priority for the furlough was to teach him how to take tablets!

38

A VOICE FROM THE PAST

Jeremy switched on the tape recorder and settled back in his seat. He listened with interest to the voice on the tape – it was a voice from the past, the voice of Stanley Benington! He heard the story of Stanley's conversion and his call to the Qua Iboe Mission. He shook his head in amazement when he realised the enormity of the journey Stanley had undertaken in the 1930s. In his mind's eye, he traced the progress of the little Ford car across most of West Africa.

"That would be a huge adventure, even by today's standards," he thought. " I'm not sure that I would be prepared to do it, even with the benefit of a four wheel drive car and proper bridges and greatly improved roads."

He wondered at the obedience of both Tigite and Stanley to God's voice and the way in which God brought them together. He could identify with many of the circumstances in which Stanley found himself and realised how wisely he had dealt with the people.

One particular incident would remain in his mind for a long time. It was the story of how Stanley had gone against his inclination to help Juremiko with food when he was hungry and instead had obeyed God's prompting to simply pray with him. Jeremy could look back on many times when he had been in the same position and knew that as long as he served God in Africa, he would feel that tension within his own heart. He prayed that he too would hear the prompting of God as clearly as Stanley had in those early days.

As he praised God for the wonderful way He had led and empowered His servant and for the marvellous way He had protected him and provided for him, Jeremy was reminded of the many times when God had poured out His love and blessing in a similar way on Rachel and himself. His soul was encouraged and refreshed and he praised God afresh for His grace.

He thought of the difficulties they had experienced in the past few months and he knew that there would be other challenges to face when they returned to Legmoin. But Jeremy had seen God at work and he was confident that the God who had been faithful to Stanley Benington as he brought the Good News of Jesus to the Lobis, would remain faithful to them in their work among the Dagari people.

He thought of his hopes and aspirations for the area around Legmoin and he remembered the map he had made for deputation. It was a map used by health care workers, showing all the villages in the area. He had copied it onto an acetate sheet and marked all the villages with a little cross – so many villages…. so much work to do!

And he dreamt of a time when all the little crosses on his map would have been reached with the Gospel: a time when the New Testament would be available to the Dagaris in their own language; a time when the literacy programme would have opened the door to the Bible for many of the Christians; a time when the Church would be strong and keen to spread the Gospel; a time when the Name of Jesus would be glorified.

What a tremendous privilege it was to be involved in this mighty task!

EPILOGUE
Angel Talk

Michael and Gabriel were puzzled.

"Why doesn't He let us do it?" Michael asked.

They were sitting in a quiet corner of Heaven, chatting together as they watched what was happening on the small but beautiful blue and green planet called Earth.

"I know, we could do a far better job." Gabriel sighed. "Those human creatures He depends on so much are really quite useless. I know He loves them but they're so disobedient. Just take, for example, that little place in Africa –Burkina Faso. I don't know how many times He spoke in someone's ear about it and none of them took any notice. They sometimes seem to be too afraid to do His will. We, on the other hand, are too afraid not to do His will and we would have started to obey even while He was still speaking!"

"And it would have been such a privilege. You know, I think He made a mistake when he gave them choice and free will. If I had been creating creatures to serve me, I would have *made* them obey me!"

"It would certainly have got the job done more efficiently. But you know," Gabriel went on, and his voice took on a rather wistful quality, "I think I can understand why He did it. Have you ever seen His smile when one of those stubborn creatures does obey Him, out of love and with no compulsion?"

Michael nodded slowly. "Yes, I've been in the Presence when that happens - it lights up Heaven. But it's just so frustrating watching them make such a mess of it all, knowing that we could do better. Even the obedient ones – they're so slow and weak and they're not very well equipped for the task. They can't fly in an instant from one place to another. It takes them ages getting anywhere in those little steel structures."

"And it takes them even longer learning a new language," Gabriel added. "At least people hear us in their own language when we speak to them. All this language learning adds years on to the job. It can be hard watching them struggle with it – funny, sometimes too!"

"Of course, to be fair, we must remember that some of them have the right idea – it just takes so long."

Gabriel smiled, "I know what you mean. Men like Stanley and Jeremy have the vision, they can see what needs to be done.........."

"Stanley and Jeremy .... we got all excited up here about their plans. Now if only He had let *us* carry out those plans. You know that map of villages that Jeremy wants to evangelise? You and I could have taken a legion or two of angels and appeared to everyone in those villages to tell them the Good News. It would have been so easy, too – job done in a couple of hours."

"The only problem with that," Gabriel reminded Michael, "is that we frighten those human creatures so easily. They're just not used to shining presences from Heaven speaking to them."

Michael laughed, "Yes, we are rather impressive, aren't we?"

Gabriel turned to him with a serious expression,

"You know I'm not sure we'll ever really understand His reasons for spreading the Gospel this way. You and I and the legions of mighty angels may be impressive and much more beautiful than the human creatures He created, but He seems to have a very special place in His heart for them. Maybe we could do a better job and do it more quickly and efficiently but He has chosen to do it through them. Somehow, seeing them serve Him, however ineffectively, brings more pleasure to Him than we ever could in an eternity of faultless service."

"He loves them with such passion, doesn't He? It must be wonderful to be loved by Him like that......" Michael gazed down at the little planet, turning in space on its axis, and looked as though he wished that he could be one of those human creatures so beloved by Heaven's King.

"Do you think they know?" Gabriel wondered. "Do you think they have any idea of the depth of His love?"

"They would if they could hear Him singing," Michael smiled. "What an amazing sound that is – when the God of Heaven rejoices over His children with singing. The hosts of heavenly choristers might sing well but even they listen with awe when the King sings over

RSW
2/9/02

BIBLIOGRAPHY

Transcripts of tape recordings made by Stanley Benington.

'The Quarterly Magazine' 1930-1937

(Public Records Office reference numbers:
D/3301/EA/14
D/3301/EA/15
D/3301/EA/16
D/3301/EA/17)

'Missionary Trails' by WG Lewis published 1937

'The Quest of Souls in Qua Iboe' by Eva Stuart Watt published 1951

'Albert Dean' by the Four Brothers Dean

Letters from Stanley and Alice Benington to Jean Corbett

'Survey of the Southern Dagari People in Burkina Faso' by Graham Cheesman 1990

Q.I.M. Quarterly 1939-1955

'Grace to Follow' by Jean Corbett